A Practical Guide to Full-Time RV Living

Motorhome & RV Retirement Startup

By

Jack Freeman

&

Shirley Freeman

Parma Books

Cover & Book Design by Rebecca Floyd

TABLE OF CONTENTS

INTRODUCTION

The freedom of the open road and retirement, two of the best things you can put together. If you raised a family, chances are those children are now adults and building lives of their own. They no longer need their parents to make them lunch or to soothe their cold or their fever; instead, your child may now seek out advice about more complex problems.

Essentially, there is no imminent economic responsibility since you are no longer feeding more individuals other than yourself (at least, that is how it goes in most situations). You may retire with a certain sense of peace of mind, knowing the world is your proverbial oyster and there are no bosses limiting your schedule, and no extra work hours needed during late nights.

Exactly six years ago my spouse Shirley and I have both retired from our previous careers, leaving us with quite a lot of extra time in a mostly empty house throughout the day. That's when we decided we wanted to travel. The problem here is we did not know what the best way was to get from point A to point B.

For one, I have the beginnings of osteoarthritis, which mostly affects my knees. While it is manageable, Shirley always suggests I should not overexert myself. For another, she is not too fond of camping on the solid ground, since it tends to make her waist ache.

Needless to say, we needed to find a way that was comfortable for the two of us, given our conditions; we did not want our sense of adventure to be limited by something as unimportant as physical pain, after all. That is when we spoke to our neighbors, old family friends who had just returned from an RV camping trip with another couple.

The more we learned about traveling in an RV, the more my wife and I were convinced that was the solution to our conundrum. We had the money, we had the time, and we could go wherever we wanted in the world with the safety aspect of carrying a piece of home with you.

Now, while having an itinerary still helps, you don't have to limit your time and be back for work. If you want to stay a few extra days to hike that extra trail or see that extra site, then you can. Retirement is a chance to get out and see the areas you never had time to when you were working.

However, RV living isn't just for retirees; it can be for anyone who wants to enjoy the freedom of living on the road although this doesn't mean that full-time RV living is for everyone.

Whether you are retiring soon and want some adventure, have been retired for a while and want a change of scene, or simply want to change your way of life to something simpler, living full-time out of an RV can be your answer.

We have been living the RV life for the last five years now, and I must admit that these five years are the best years of our life so far. I also must admit that not everything was glorious and fun, yes, we have faced our fair share of problems and hiccups on various fronts, but at the end of the looking back, they all were great learning experiences.

In this book, we are going to show you what is involved in RV living, how you can get started and what you need to do to live an affordable full-time life on the road while enjoying the wonderful sights. So let's get started and take a look at whether or not this lifestyle is right for you.

IS RV LIVING RIGHT FOR YOU?

Living full-time in a motorhome, travel trailer, or camper is an appealing option to many but isn't for everyone. In order to determine if this lifestyle is right for you, you need to give it some serious thought and look into all the pros and cons involved before making a final decision. Some factors that may influence your choice include the following:

☐ Age

☐ Health

☐ Family Situation

- ☐ Mechanical Ability

- ☐ Finances

- ☐ Emotional and Physical Ability

Some of the reasons that people decide to live in an RV full-time include the following. Do any of them apply to you?

- ☐ Travel without reservations.

- ☐ Moving between places easily and at a low-cost.

- ☐ A greater sense of freedom.

- ☐ Increased flexibility.

- ☐ More free time.

These are all good reasons to live full-time on the road, but a lot of these reasons are based on assumptions. Before you jump into full-time RV living it is important that you consider the facts. Consider the truth of the three biggest assumptions about life on the road.

First, people believe the fact that full-time RV living is cheaper than owning or renting a home or apartment. However, as we will see when we discuss costs later, depending on the choices a person makes, living in an RV can actually be more costly. From maintenance to actually acquiring one, that is.

Second, many people think that living in an RV is a very freeing experience that will always be enjoyable. However, not everyone can adapt to living in a small space, and it can actually be more difficult than you realize given the limitations you are given in those quarters. It might also be rough for those who suffer from sensitive motion sickness, as they would be spending most of the time on the road or in a moving vehicle as they explore a country or state.

Lastly, people think that living in an RV is an easy and carefree lifestyle. However, it is important to know that have a recreational vehicle requires a lot of constant care and upkeep in order to avoid major and costly problems, as well as extremely solid planning.

Finding gas stations, figuring out where to stay overnight, coming up with places to eat or how to handle the food situation, knowing what to do in an emergency, having the proper documents and license registration information, being prepared for any possibility that the RV begins to malfunction, all of these factors are relevant.

These three reasons show why it is important to consider the pros and cons of living in an RV full-time. Let's look at those first, shall we?

PROS AND CONS OF FULL-TIME RV LIVING

Living on the road isn't all it is cracked up to be, but it isn't the worst lifestyle choice you can make. As a retiree, you probably already have a home or are in a position to own a home or an apartment somewhere. This is why we will carefully consider both the pros and cons to see which apply to you and make sure living in an RV is truly something beneficial for you.

PROS OF HOME OWNERSHIP

Owning a home or living in a house offers more benefits than you may be aware of at the moment. Consider the benefits you can have from homeownership:

- Location stability.

- An investment that will grow over time.

- A way to increase personal wealth.

- Affords privacy to everyone who lives there.

- Often provides more than one bedroom and bathroom, along with space for storage or a workshop as needed.

- Gives you extra rooms for guests or a decent-sized place to prepare a meal for others.

- Provides you with a yard if you have pets or grandchildren who visit.

- The pride of home ownership.

- A place where you can build memories.

In addition to these benefits, for a retiree, a home comes with some additional long term benefits. As you age, certain comforts are important, and a house allows you to make the necessary adjustments so you can continue to live longer on your own before requiring assistance.

For example, a home gives you room to have a bed that accommodates your needs. Another ability is to widen doorways as needed to accommodate medical equipment like walkers and wheelchairs. Plus you have the option to renovate bathrooms for handicap access. These types of changes and improvements can't be done in an RV. Plus the equity in a home will give you some assistance in the event of a medical emergency.

This isn't to say that owning a home isn't without its drawbacks. Let's look at some of the cons of home ownership.

CONS OF HOME OWNERSHIP

Having a home can be expensive with additional costs for labor and repairs, particularly if you intend to repair an older model or if it has unexpected issues with plumbing, leaks, or any other structural issues. Plus you need to put in a lot of labor to maintain it, which can also be time-consuming, giving you less time to enjoy the retirement lifestyle.

- Owning a home comes with added expenses that are often increasing such as mortgage, tax, and insurance. Your retirement income often doesn't increase with these costs so you'll be left wondering if you can afford your home as the year's pass.

- You are pretty much stuck in one area. While you can choose to go on a vacation, your time is limited to your finances, and then you need to return home. Plus you need to make sure the home is kept up while you are gone unless you already have a trusted contact or family member who is willing to help in this matter.

- In some areas, a home can lose value, which means you'll have a difficult time selling your home if you want to move. Sometimes if moving is necessary, you'll be taking a loss on the amount you paid for your home due to depreciation.

- If there are ever any rising costs or unforeseen medical expenses you could end up losing your home. This would mean losing all the investment and time you've put into your home as well.

These can be powerful motivators and reasons for choosing whether or not moving into life on the road is right for you. Now let's take a look at what to consider when it comes to living in an RV.

PROS OF LIVING IN AN RV

Perhaps one of the main reasons people are drawn to living in an RV is the financial benefits. Depending on the choices you make while living in an RV, there can certainly be savings that offset any loss of owning and maintaining an RV. For example, if you live in an RV you can save on the following:

- No property taxes.

- No homeowners' insurance.

- Less cost for electricity.

- No cost for sewer and water.

- Potentially free access to internet and TV if you know where to look.

- Less need to spend money on tools and cleaning products.

- No need to spend money on furniture.

- Greater control over your living costs.

In addition to these potential financial savings, there are other benefits to living in an RV full-time. Some of these benefits include the following, but see if you can think of others that apply to you:

- You are able to travel more and explore wherever you want under the proper requirements of the place you are visiting.

- You can live more minimally with less physical and mental clutter.

- When you downsize, you can sell things and increase your retirement savings.

- You have complete freedom and flexibility so you can move where you want when you want.

- You are able to get closer to nature without having to "rough it up."

- If your family doesn't live nearby, you can travel to visit them easily.

- Traveling in an RV can actually be safer for retirees than a house since neighbors are closer by and most campgrounds have good security.

- In the event of natural disasters, it is easy to simply drive away and go somewhere else away from the danger.

- Many RV parks and campgrounds come with free amenities that allow you to live the fully retired resort lifestyle.

- Modern RVs are more comfortable and homelike.

- If you are traveling in your RV, it is easier since you don't have to worry about packing or potentially leaving something behind.

- A smaller living area is easier to care for.

- Lastly, less space means less chance for injuries such as falls.

There are quite a few benefits involved in owning an RV. However, this isn't to say it doesn't come with drawbacks, just like owning a home. Let's look at some of the reasons why living in an RV may not be right for you, or why it would need a few modifications if it is still something you may want.

CONS OF LIVING IN AN RV

When you consider all the benefits above it may seem like a great idea to sell your house, buy an RV, and head out on the open road. Living in an RV may seem like the ideal situation, but as we covered, it may not be the best option for every individual based on their preferences and current lifestyle. Some of the cons consist of:

- It is not near family.

- Continuous maintenance and upkeep is required.

- Repairs can add up quickly.

- Space is very limited.

- Traveling can be expensive depending on your tastes and needs.

- You still have monthly fees for things like RV payments, licenses, insurance, campsite, and utilities.

- Safety can be an issue unless you take proper precautions and stay in the right kind of RV spots.

- Depending on where you travel, gas can be quite expensive.

- No dedicated doctor for medical needs.

- Difficult internet and satellite reception in some areas, limiting communication.

- Temperature control can be difficult.

- Finding long term campsites and places to park is difficult.

- Privacy is limited.

After considering the drawbacks to living in an RV full-time, you may be hesitating. Perhaps one of the biggest questions you are asking yourself is the same thing I asked myself, what if it doesn't work out?

There is a lot of thought involved, and most of it comes down to your personal situation and desires. Oftentimes, either choice you make is going to be mostly permanent because it can be difficult to go back.

Therefore, a good piece of advice is to be cautious and maybe consider renting or borrowing an RV for a few trips and see if you feel like it is something you can do full-time or if it is something you prefer as an occasional type of thing. Here are some questions to take in mind.

FIVE QUESTIONS TO ASK BEFORE STARTING FULL-TIME RV LIVING

If you are still on the fence about living in an RV, then consider the following five questions. These can help you think about and evaluate your current situation.

What Attracts You to RV Living?

Are you attracted to RV living because you get to travel to destinations you've always wanted to visit? Are you interested in traveling from place to place to stay where the weather is nice, and you are closer to your family?

Before you determine whether or not this is right for you, you need to establish the "why." That will also help if you hit hard times while on the road since you will be able to focus on the "why" to keep you going and have the strength to make it through regardless of the circumstances.

What Is Currently Making You Unhappy?

Is there something in your life that is making you unhappy? Do you feel unfulfilled and unsettled in your day to day life? Do you want more than your standard routine? Do you need a change in life and want to live life your way? Think about your current situation and what is prompting you to consider full-time RV living.

What Is Causing Your Unhappiness?

Determining what is making you unhappy is important, but you also want to determine the actual cause of your unhappiness. Living on the road in an RV is a great solution to a lot of things, but it won't solve all problems.

Not all your problems are going to be solved overnight or instantly resolved when you start living out of an RV. There is a difference between running away from difficult situations and addressing them before beginning a new journey.

It is true that you'll have a life that is different from the routine day to day existence. It is true that you'll be able to spend more time doing what you want and spending more quality time with your significant other. However, if part of your unhappiness is sharing a space with your significant other, moving into an RV together is not likely to resolve the relationship dysfunctionalities unless they are previously discussed in an open environment.

Try to carefully and openly think about what gives you a sense of disheartened thoughts or less energy and evaluate whether or not moving into an RV is going to alleviate or worsen any previous resentments, tensions, or arguments.

Are You Willing to Put Up with the Cons?

As you have seen from the lists above, living in an RV isn't all the hype it is set up to be. While it is a great lifestyle and there are many benefits, you need to be willing to make a few sacrifices to gain the benefits. You'll have to make some changes and sacrifices in order to start life on the road.

You'll have to sell things and downsize your belongings. Ask yourself if you are willing to do whatever it takes in order to start your life of living on the road full-time, and if you are doing it as a personal choice and desire, or as a way to avoid your responsibilities or prior issues.

Can You Handle...?

Similar to the last question: this is about whether or not you can make a few sacrifices to change your lifestyle. For some these situations may be more challenging than others and how challenging it is for you will determine how well life on the road is going to be for you. At the very least you want to think of these situations and how you'll handle them when transitioning to living in an RV.

...Living in a Small Space?

For many, the living space in an RV is substantially smaller than what most are used to. Downsizing and living in such a small space is often one of the most challenging adjustments for people. How do you envision yourself handling this? How do you currently use the space in your home? Do you have a special area that you find yourself going to get away from others?

It may be hard to tell how you will do in a smaller living space, but if you need personal space to be comfortable, there will need to be further adjustments in order to make it work without the situation exploding at some point. There could be established quiet times where you are able to do things like reading, writing, or simply relaxing in complete silence without being worried about any interruptions.

But that depends on your partner in case, and whether they can respect those set boundaries, and if you can respect theirs as well.

...Living with Fewer Possessions?

It is obvious that you won't have room for many possessions while living in an RV. You'll likely have to give up a lot of modern conveniences, and you'll have to change or adjust a lot of your daily activities. Ask yourself if you can do without amenities such as a dishwasher, laundry machines, or a bathtub. What would you do if you couldn't have all the clothes you have now?

For many, this may seem difficult, but after the downsizing process, many people find that living with fewer possessions is actually one of the best pros to living in an RV. When you live with less, you are able to experience more since you aren't held back by physical items that you do not even need in order to be happy.

However, this isn't always the case for every individual so you'll need to think about how important possessions are before you set out to live in an RV since you will definitely not be able to take everything you own with you. Then again, this is the perfect opportunity to donate those new shirts that have stuffed in your closet but rarely ever wear or those shoes you bought for special occasions only to realize there aren't many of those happening in recent years.

Learning how to let go of items that do not matter is an extremely worthwhile growing experience that allows you to truly hold value in key items; into the ones that really can never be replaced.

...A Lack of Routine?

One of the main draws to RV life is the chance to be free and not be confined by a static routine, but then again, perhaps you thoroughly enjoy that routine. Living on the road means that one day won't be the same as the next. For some, this is new and exciting, while for others it means instability and emotionally-draining contexts. When traveling full-time, it can be difficult to develop a routine in even simple matters such as cooking a meal.

Ask yourself how you handle change and if you view yourself as patient and flexible, as well as someone who can develop relatively solid plans where it matters. These are traits that can make it easier to adapt to full-time living in an RV.

Make sure you give careful thought to the pros and cons as well as the questions addressed above, this will help you see if you should give full-time RV living a try. If you do think it is for you, then keep reading. Next, we're going to consider the costs of full-time RV living so you can make sure you are financially ready for the transition.

HOW MUCH DOES IT COST TO RV FULL-TIME

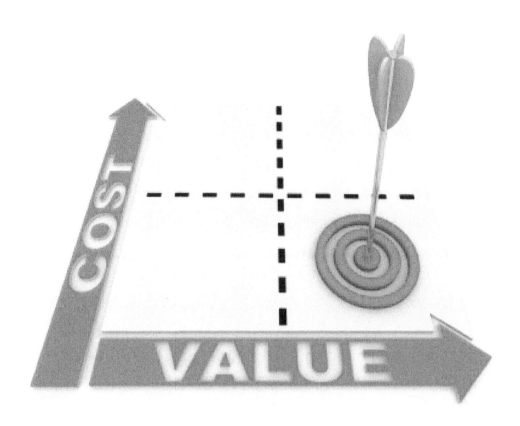

In general, living in an RV is going to save you money on the daily costs of living. For some, RV living is a financially-beneficial decision. However, it may not be as cheap as you think. Therefore, let's take the time to consider the cost of living in an RV full-time to make sure you can afford it before you get started.

CONSIDER THESE ELEVEN COSTS

The costs you need to consider when determining if RV living is right for you will largely depend on your lifestyle and individual choices. If you prefer to stay at sites that have full hookups only, then you can expect to pay a bit more.

If you want to stay in one area for a longer period of time, then you are likely to spend less money because of extended stay discounts. I'm going to discuss some of the typical costs associated with RV living and their average pricing schemes, but keep in mind your individual situation may be different, so these numbers are not stagnant.

RV COSTS

If you are financing your RV, be sure to include the cost of payments. This will vary depending on the financial arrangement you reach with your supplier.

Even if your RV is still under warranty, you should still consider the cost of maintenance and repair by setting aside some money each month. This can help go towards things that aren't covered under warranty such as oil changes, water filters, wiper blades, and general maintenance. Ideally, you should try to set aside $50 to $100 a month for a repairs and maintenance budget.

Depending on the dealership where you purchase your RV, the suppliers may or may not provide some of the basics needed to live and travel from an RV. However, there will probably be some gear and/or modifications you want to make, so the RV is more comfortable or safer for you.

For example, you may want to outfit your RV with solar panels for a boondocking or off-the-grid living. This can actually be an ongoing expense that you'll save for and purchase over time. Again, these costs will be determined by what comes included with your RV purchase and which things you want to change for your own personal benefit and comfort.

If you are going to be living in your RV full-time, you definitely want to have RV insurance. This helps protect your RV and its contents, but we'll talk more about this a bit later. If you are financing your RV, make sure you are covered for the full payoff amount. The average RV insurance with a tow car is $145 a month.

A big part of your budget is going to be saved for the fuel. However, this cost will also vary by how far you drive and how often you change locations. Despite these changes, you may expect about $300 to $500 a month in total for gas expenses.

Depending on where you travel you may also need to take into account the cost of toll roads, which are becoming increasingly more commonplace in the United States. Look to see if there is a way to minimize cost with passes in areas you frequent more than others.

Your annual registration fees are going to be determined by your legal state of residence. For some states this is free, and in others, you'll be paying property taxes based on the value of your RV.

Most RVs use propane appliances such as stoves, ovens, refrigerators, or heaters. This means you'll need to budget for having propane in hand as well. RV travelers tend to spend an average of $5 and $40 a month on propane gas.

Similarly, if you have a generator and you use it, you'll want to set a budget for that kind of fuel. If you stay at full hookup campgrounds, you may not use your generator as often as if you decided to go off on your own while skipping those stops.

However, when you are staying at non-hookup locations, you may have to purchase fuel to keep things like your air conditioning running, which is particularly important during the hotter seasons of the places you visit.

Tow Vehicle Costs

If you choose to tow a vehicle behind your RV, you'll need to take the following associated costs into account as well.

As with the RV, make sure you account for any vehicle payments you have, and you will need to set aside a little bit of money each month to help cover the cost of maintenance and repairs as well as the insurance coverage.

A towed vehicle may come with additional gear and/or modifications such as a towing package.

As you can imagine, a tow vehicle is also going to need fuel. This is a variable cost since it depends on how many days you drive it and how far you travel while staying in one place. It also depends on your tow vehicle and what gas mileage it gets.

Storage Costs

Even if you downsize your life and move into an RV full-time, you may still want to save some items for future use. If this is the case, then you'll likely put them in a storage unit. If you do this, make sure you include the rental costs in your monthly budget as well.

Campground Costs

This is going to be one of your biggest recurring expenses, but it will heavily depend on your lifestyle and type of RV living. The following are some general categories to consider–keep in mind that each one comes with its own variables. We'll also discuss more about the types of places to stay in your RV later in this guide.

Resort campgrounds offer you numerous perks. These locations are going to cost you extra based on amenities, location, and time of travel. The typical cost for resort campgrounds can vary between $30 to $50 a night or about $900 to $1,500 a month.

National and State Parks don't have many amenities or full hookups but are often located in beautiful locations. Again the cost can vary, but it is often less than resort campgrounds. However, they are in higher demand so it can be harder to get a reservation at these sites. They can typically cost between $15 to $28 a night or about $360 to $600 a month.

Lastly, boondocking is the process of camping without hookups in random locations for free or under $15 a night. There are plenty of spaces to do this in the United States. I will tell you that the majority of boondocking sites are in the west and they get less plentiful the further east you travel due to weather conditions and complications surrounding that.

FOOD COSTS

Oftentimes, this cost won't vary much from month to month. If you prefer to eat out a lot, this will likely continue as you live in an RV. There are two main category costs for food.

Groceries is the cost of any food you want to have on hand. This number can vary slightly since the price can change by region and sometimes food is higher priced when it is located near cities or popular tourist areas. Taxes will also vary by location. You may also want to include personal care items in this category as well since you often purchase them along with your groceries. This includes vitamins, medicines you are previously instructed to take, herbal teas, and items such as shampoo or soap or toilet paper.

You also want to have a category for eating out. Even if you prefer to make the majority of your meals yourself, you'll probably still want to sample local restaurants in the area from time to time. This is one section of your budget where you have complete control.

If you lack the money to eat out in one of those occasions, you can always save it by staying in your RV and making your own food, so regardless you should always carry some form of canned or pre-frozen meals in case of emergencies (being unable to purchase more groceries, and being unable to eat out for the time being).

INSURANCE COST

Health insurance costs can vary greatly depending on your declared state of residence, the size of your family, and the type of coverage you want. When you start RV living full-time, you should take the time to research your state of residence and pick one that offers you the best rates.

Life insurance is one area that many people choose to cut since it helps save cost. However, if you are in fairly good health, you should consider life insurance since it isn't that expensive and will help your family should something happen to you. You should at least have enough insurance to pay for funeral and burial costs, plus enough to cover any outstanding debts you may have so they are not passed on to your family.

While this is a morbid sort of topic to consider or to talk about, the sooner it is taken care of, the better. If you do not intend to have a typical funeral, or do not intend to be buried (but rather opt for being cremated), that lessens expenses, which is another factor to take in mind. Then again, this is something left entirely to personal preference.

There could already be a family plot, or perhaps another formerly-established tradition based on religion or cultural customs. Regardless, just make sure those factors are taken care of ahead of time.

MAIL SERVICE COSTS

Most people who live full-time from an RV tend to do as much of their mail electronically as possible, but there are still going to be some things that need to be mailed. There is the option to use the stable address of a family member, but you can also choose to use a mailing service such as a P.O. Box. If you use a mailing service make sure you add this to your monthly budget. The average cost of this is about $16 to $20 depending on the service package you choose.

LAUNDRY COSTS

If your RV doesn't come with a washer and dryer, you will need to include a laundry cost in your monthly budget. Depending on the number of loads you do per month and the size of the machines you use, you can expect your laundry budget to be about $18 to $20 per month. You will need to add the expenses of laundry detergent and a laundry bag as well as a fabric softener (if you use it) and bleach.

Another option is to wash your clothes by hand if you are really not interested in those numbers and you happen to have very sturdy clothes accompanied by a hands-on disposition.

ELECTRONICS COSTS

There are a few things to consider under the electronics budget. This can include your cost for internet service, cell phones, television coverage, and any streaming subscriptions.

Cell phone service can vary depending on where you are in the country. It is best to review various plans and find ones with the best coverage in the area you plan to travel. Then factor the cost into your monthly budget.

Depending on your need for internet access you may want to purchase a hotspot or other devices that come with a monthly plan so you can have internet access no matter where you are. However, many resort campgrounds often have internet available. In some places, the internet can be spotty at best. So consider how reliable you want your coverage to be for your intents and purposes.

Another electronic you may want to consider is satellite TV. Some resort campgrounds will offer cable, but if you are boondocking or staying in a park, then you'll want to consider a satellite service to keep watching TV. Of course, this also depends on how much TV you watch; you may just prefer spending your time exploring the great outdoors.

Lastly, you may want to pay for streaming subscriptions. There are many to choose from, and you can choose them based on your viewing preferences. Whatever you choose, make sure you include them in your monthly budget.

My personal recommendation is, even if you are the sort who watches a lot of television or scrolls aimlessly through social media platforms, turn off the screen, put on your walking shoes, and step outside to the world in front of you.

There comes a time when no soap opera, no rerun, no movie can truly compare to the life you could have if you only decide to take that first step of owning it and talking to the very-much real people in it.

Any shows can wait in comparison to standing in front of a 134-foot waterfall crashing against the rocks, or staring at the starry sky, and every constellation is spread out before you or learning about the history of any place you go through cultural festivals, museums, and visitor centers.

You cannot truly look at the world from behind a television screen or a cell phone lens or a gleaming bright blue display. I was able to hug and kiss my wife under the Golden Gate Bridge as we went through San Francisco and impulsively hopped on a ferry surrounding Alcatraz Island.

It was so chilly we were shivering from under our coats, and we kept getting sprayed with cold sea foam from the waves, but that moment of seeing the bottom of such a historic structure is something that sticks out in my memory more than any episode of any show I used to save up hours of my week for.

After the ferry, we walked to a small hole-in-the-wall restaurant with the best fettuccine Alfredo with crab, lobster, and shrimp I have ever tasted in my life. I am not saying to close off all devices since we love watching a movie at the end of a long day as much as the next person.

All I am saying is to focus on paying a small amount of money on a simple streaming device rather than a full-scale satellite TV dish since you should not feel the urge to stay indoors for hours on end, neither at your home nor in an RV.

PET COSTS

If you have pets that are going to travel with you, they are going to have their own associated costs. Be sure to budget their monthly food and veterinarian expenses as well.

Often the cost for these services is going to be pretty much the same as what you paid before you started living in an RV, so you should be able to carry on without much trouble and have your furry best friend curled up at your feet during the night.

ENTERTAINMENT COSTS

While you'll be living in an RV and having fun and freedom each day, you may still want to explore new places, naturally. Therefore, make sure to leave room in your monthly budget for fun costs such as admission to amusement parks, museums, farmers' markets, national parks, and other facilities.

Depending on your lifestyle, you may also want to consider things like movies or hotels and B&Bs in your budget in case you want to take a break from the RV lifestyle on occasion.

CAN YOU AFFORD TO LIVE FULL-TIME IN AN RV?

Now that I've talked to you about the costs that go into full-time RV living, I want to talk to you about determining whether or not you can afford to live in an RV in the first place. With the right planning and budgeting, you are able to live in an RV for cheap and save a lot of money, which is why cost control is one of the main benefits of this decision.

However, transferring from your home into an RV will not solve your economic difficulties overnight, since there are more steps to take in order to achieve financial stability under these conditions. This is why it is important to read a guide on the matter; it will help you to consider the real cost of this lifestyle as well as ways to save money.

AVERAGE RV LIVING COSTS

So let's truly answer the question: how expensive is it going to be to live in an RV? The truth is there is no easy way to answer this. I know, I know, you may be slightly irritated at that unsatisfactory response, but it really does depend on your own decisions and whether they are cost-effective.

As you see above there is a wide spectrum to all aspects of RV living–from the RV you choose, the foods you eat, and the locations you visit No matter what your current budget or how much money you are going to save up, you are sure to find an RV lifestyle that meets your needs. All you need to do is take a little time to plan.

LIVING AFFORDABLY IN AN RV

RV living is the best combination of freedom and a minimalist lifestyle. This combination is key to a cheap and frugal way of living if you do things right. On the other hand, it is entirely possible that you end up burning through your savings faster than you thought and find yourself looking for odd jobs to stay afloat.

The key to affording life in an RV is to first determine the right RV for your retirement and travel lifestyle. RV prices tend to go from $10,000 to $300,000 depending on what exactly you are willing to attain. I went for one that was roughly $11,100 since other than my knees and her waist, my wife and I don't actually have any imminent medical conditions that require modifications or extra comfort.

I just need a warm place to sit and rest from time to time, and she just needs a specific type of foam mattress, so a wheelchair or handicap modifications and the like should be a major factor to include in pricing if you or your partner need them. It does help quite a bit that you do not need to pay the full price in one hard hit, but can rather split it into monthly payments with a special plan or package.

There could also be certain discounts or opportunities, particularly if you know of someone who wants to sell their RV or if you choose a used one that has everything you need in mint condition. Then you can choose the most affordable model.

Once you have your ideal RV, you can look at where you want to go first, and you can customize your options based on your budget. This will take care of the two biggest variable costs: campgrounds and fuel.

BUDGETING FOR RV LIVING

When it comes to staying at an RV site, you can easily pay $500 or more a month for a fancy spot with all the amenities you can think of. However, you can also spend less than $25 for two weeks at a public campground. You can even choose to boondock and find places to camp for free.

Basically, the point is that you can RV for cheap if you avoid paying for hookups and do a little extra research before heading to a location. We'll discuss more about boondocking later, but with proper planning, you can boondock for cheap and still live a comfortable life on the road. No matter what your lifestyle preference, you should create a budget worksheet when switching to full-time RV living so you know how much you can afford in all of the categories we discussed earlier.

FOUR STEPS TO AFFORDING FULL-TIME RV LIVING

In order to make sure you are financially ready I'm going to tell you four steps, you can take in order not to be scrambling around for money at the last minute.

CREATE A TRAVEL BUDGET

After you've purchased your RV, you need to create a monthly budget. Just as you would in a home, you need to think about necessary spending each month and work within those established numbers. As we discussed above, some of the fixed expenses that should be included in your monthly budget include the following:

- RV Payments

- Miscellaneous

- Food

- Gas

- Propane

- Laundry

- Campground Site Fees

- Internet

- Health Insurance

- Clothing

- Phone

- Household Items

- RV Insurance

- RV Maintenance and Repairs

LOOK FOR WAYS TO REDUCE COST

There are many ways to reduce costs, save money, and afford full-time RV living. This doesn't mean you have to be rigorously micro-managing everything you do and spend, though. Most people who live from an RV can have an affordable budget and still be able to enjoy their time on the road.

While I'll discuss money saving options in greater details towards the end of this book, let's look at a few ways to save money so you can see how possible it is.

- When choosing a place to stay, go for those that only offer the amenities you plan to use. Think of it this way: the more amenities a park has, the more costly it is going to be. For example, you don't want to pay extra for a campground or RV park that has a swimming pool if you don't plan on going swimming while there. Same goes for a Jacuzzi or horseback riding trails

Fuel consumption can be reduced with planning, traveling at the posted speed limits, and not going over your pre-established driving goals during the day.

- Reduce your spending on impulse purchases that aren't in the budget. It can be easy to limit your purchases since an RV can't hold a lot of possessions, but the general questions to ask yourself when making extra purchases are:

1. Do you really need that item?

2. Is the item worth its price, or could you find it somewhere else a lot cheaper?

3. Are you willing to bend other parts of your budget in order to make up for buying the item?

Now, these are only questions to consider if your purchase in the case is particularly expensive and if you are on a tight sort of economic situation. If you have completed all the necessary payments and went a little under what you normally pay and have some leftover cash for the month, you don't need to worry about much regardless. If you can afford it without jeopardizing your more important monthly payments, it is always healthy to splurge a little bit from time to time.

- Meal preparation is key to budgeting and making proper use of space. Shop local markets for seasonal and fresh items, prepare your meals and cook them as needed. This will not only help with healthier eating, but it will also reduce the cost of eating out all the time. While eating out may be more convenient, it will certainly have a bigger impact on your budget. Like with the item purchases, you may always save an extra slot in your budget for a monthly dinner somewhere nice, so you and your partner can have a date and taste the cuisine of the place you are visiting.

EARN SIDE INCOME

If you are only semi-retired and are living in an RV, then you can find some side jobs that help you cover the costs of your travels. You have choices when it comes to seasonal and part-time jobs at campgrounds, national parks, and even online jobs you can do from your computer in the comfort of your RV.

I can still do cartoon commissions while working on a graphic novel, and all I need is my digital drawing pad and internet from time to time. As for my wife, she gets some pocket money by selling extra resin pendants she made before our decision to live in the RV and keeps making woven copper wire jewelry for the people in the B&Bs we sometimes stay at. It is simple work that keeps us busy during the days we are not feeling up for too much walking or exploring.

You may also do online freelance work if you are interested in photography, writing, blogging, video editing, translating, and so many more categories available. There are even websites nowadays where you can teach English to people from all over the world from the comfort of your phone or your laptop, and you are in control of your own schedule.

Doing these four things will have you financially prepared for life in an RV. Let's look at the steps you need to take to prepare yourself for life on the road.

PREPARING FOR FULL-TIME LIFE ON THE ROAD

Having life on the road is growing in popularity, but it still isn't what others would call their exact definition of normal. If you've taken the time to set down roots in a home, it can be difficult to uproot everything and start a far different lifestyle on the road.

To some, it may even come as a shock to not officially have a single rooted place to come back to at the end of the day. Needless to say, preparing for life on the road isn't easy, but it is well worth it if it is what you are looking for. You just need to take it one step at a time, and you'll be successful before you know it.

Let's look at some tips I learned that helped me transition to living on the road.

ESTABLISH A DATE

Before you get into the details of transitioning to life on the road, you should establish a departure date. This may seem odd; after all, how can you know how long it will take you to prepare? Honestly, you won't know exactly how long it will take, but if you provide yourself with a deadline, then you'll have something to work for. Without a set date then you won't have that sense of urgency, and you'll just keep talking about it rather than taking a decisive course of action.

The time you give yourself will depend on your current lifestyle. If you already own a home, you'll need to decide if you want to sell or keep it and rent it out to someone. If you are going to sell it, you need time to prepare your house for sale, which can take a little more time depending on how much work you need to do and if there are willing buyers sooner than anticipated.

You don't necessarily need to set a final departure date that is exact down to the minute of the day of the month of the year. My recommendation is to narrow it down to a year and a month for the sake of visualizing the milestones you need to cover. These milestones consist of when you want to purchase the RV, or when you want to start selling or renting out your house.

The first to-do list you develop is going to be a long one, but it is important that you write everything down that you need. A good place to start is with the following:

☐ Research Trailers

☐ Research Domicile Residency

☐ Start Downsizing

☐ Hold a Garage Sale

☐ Research Health Care

☐ Establish a Travel Destination

☐ Set a Tentative Budget

☐ Research Places to Stay

☐ Choose a Mail Service

☐ Cancel Utilities

Your to-do list may vary since each person is going to have a unique situation. Basically you want to take a moment to put together a list of what it takes for you to uproot from your current lifestyle and get out on the road. As you finish items on your list, you'll be learning more about the requirements so you'll also be able to grow your list and make it more detailed.

SIMPLIFY YOUR LIFE

Simplifying your life is something that will require a little bit of effort every single day in order for it to amount to a mountain's worth of work in a shorter period of time. What you choose to get rid of is going to be based on your plans.

If you want to travel for just a year to try it out and then return home, you'll likely want to put a lot of stuff in storage and sell only a few items. On the other hand, if you've already given it a try and know you want to go for the full-time route, you'll want to get rid of the majority of items you own and only keep the basic necessities that fit in your RV or the more sentimental items somewhere safe.

After you've started the process, you need to think carefully about things as you go begin to declutter. Decluttering can be both emotionally and physically draining, especially if you are trying to get rid of nearly everything you own and you are attached to most of your possessions.

In the end, it will be very liberating when you find you are able to keep things to a minimum and keep a sense of value to the things and the memories that matter, such as your children's art pieces, or your family heirlooms. We'll get into decluttering and downsizing in greater detail shortly.

It is going to be difficult to examine what you need to live comfortably in your RV without going down the Mrs. Potato Head route and bringing with you every single possible item for the 'what if?' scenario. Some of those scenarios are valid, but others are way too specific and extremely unlikely to happen, so that item may only take up space of something you actually need more imminently.

After I decluttered, I was surprised how little I really needed. Other than our book collection and a few things of emotional value, I found I did not need much other than my wife and our Great Dane. Any larger items that I did not want to part with (because I intended to gift to our children and friends at some point), we set up in storage.

For instance, I did not realize how many shirts and pants I did not even wear anymore but still had buried in my closet, or how many trinkets we had accumulated over the years even though they did not have any emotional value.

Just remember that a part of the process involves making mistakes, no matter how much you plan and analyze in the downsizing phase. What matters here is that you are able to adapt to these mistakes relatively quickly and not linger too much on them.

Clothing Needs

How much clothing you keep in your RV will largely depend on where you are going to travel. Most people who live in an RV full-time tend to follow the weather. If you are always staying in a mild climate, then you won't need many thick and heavy clothes, but should still have a heavy coat, a medium coat, and a couple of light sweaters available in case those predictions change during your trip, and you still want to roll with the punches.

Generally, the key to a thorough RV wardrobe is to choose clothes that can go good together and choose ones that are easy to layer. If you consider the clothes you currently have, you probably only wear about 20 percent of them. So keep the ones you wear the most and get rid of the rest. Alternatively, you could simply get new clothes similar to the ones you wear the most in order to have a more durable set.

Kitchen Needs

Consider what tools you use most in your kitchen and the ones you can't do without. Then look at the room you have available in your trailer. It may be a good idea to read up on the section on cooking in your RV later in this guide to help you see what type of cooking you're likely to do so you can tailor your utensil needs.

There are plenty of RV organizations and clubs that will make it easier to start RV living. Most of these organizations will not only give you a discount on campgrounds, but they will also help you access insider information from those who already live in RVs and can help you avoid the most common mistakes. Consider a few good options:

Escapees RV Club. Has an annual fee of $40, and it gives you up to 50 percent off in about 1,000 campgrounds. It also offers an excellent forum for RVing information as well as a mail service.

Good Sam Club. This club gives you 10 percent off at about 2,000 campgrounds. Plus it also gives you a gas discount at Pilot or Flying J gas station at five to eight cents off per gallon. Lastly, it gives you a 30 percent off discount at Camping World. All this for a $27 annual membership.

Passport America. This club allows you to save up to 50 percent off at nearly 2,000 campgrounds in the United States, Canada, and Mexico. All for a $44 annual fee.

Before you join any RV clubs, you should look closely at the fine print. Most campgrounds don't accept any type of club discounts on weekends or holidays. Plus you want to pay close attention to which campgrounds are a part of the network. Make sure they are at places you would want to stay and offering amenities you would use.

INCREASING YOUR CHANCES OF SUCCESS

Before we go further into the details and steps to transitioning your life, let's look at some tips that can help ensure you are successful.

HAVE A VISION BOARD

There is going to come the point where you are ready to give up on the process. In order to overcome this obstacle when it arises, you should have a vision board. This will help you reach your goals and stay motivated when you are ready to give up.

It is a simple method: cut out some pictures from magazines or print ones off the internet that show the life you want to have while living in your RV and make a collage on a large poster board of the places you want to visit. Then you can look at this board and remind yourself of the literal big picture representing why you are doing what you are doing, and this will help you stay focused, so you don't get too overwhelmed.

TAKE A TRIAL RUN

Before your final transition date, you should take any opportunity available to go on a trial run. The longer you can stay out in your RV the more you are going to learn. A trial run helps you determine exactly what you need to keep and what you need to take with you. This will help make the downsizing process easier.

Also once you move into your RV full-time, you may want to stay in your area for a few weeks to months so you can get used to RV life before you have to go somewhere unfamiliar. Perhaps you can rent an RV from a friend or a company and take it out for a week to a state you have yet to visit but are interested in checking out, and see for yourself if it is an arrangement you would like to make permanent.

STAY CLOSE TO FAMILY AND FRIENDS

Living on the road means you are going to lose contact with family and friends for a while as you drive between cities or stay at national parks with spotty WiFi. Therefore, when you first start you want to make time to spend with family and friends as much as possible, or you give them a heads-up, so they do not get too worried about your lack of communication with them.

Don't spend time visiting everyone at the last minute since this will take time away from the transitioning process itself and will leave you feeling stressed and exhausted. Remember: as a part of your transitioning process, you'll also want to prepare a way to keep in contact with people while you're on the road.

DEVELOP A PAPERLESS SYSTEM

The easiest way to adjust to life on the road is by going to a paperless or paper-reduced lifestyle. Since all mail is going to be forwarded from a mail service, it can be easy for bills to become overdue. Avoid this and other problems by signing up for e-billing for anything you can. Banks, utility bills, magazines, anything you receive on paper typically has an online option.

Now that we have discussed these topics very lightly, so you have a better idea of what to expect let's get into the actual steps and process of transitioning to life on the road.

5 STEP TRANSITION TO FULL-TIME RV TRAVEL

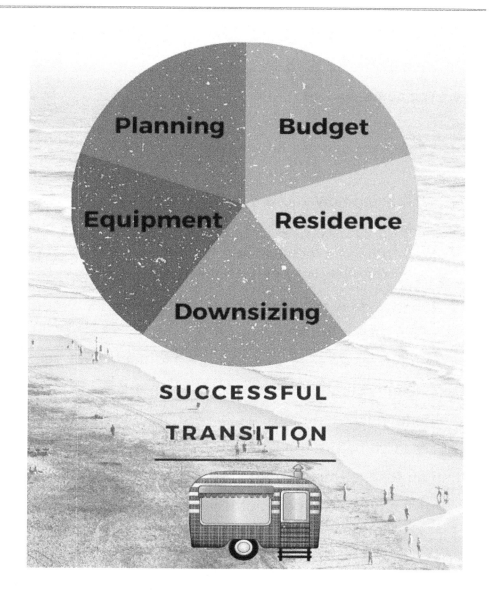

Now let's get into the actual process of transitioning to full-time RV travel. Let's go over this one step at a time.

Transitioning to full-time RV living takes a lot of planning since there are many issues that can arise. Some of the issues you'll have to deal with include the following:

- The costs involved.

- Equipment choices and purchases.

- Where and how you are going to live.

- How to handle logistics and utilities.

- What to do with everything you don't need anymore.

Some items you are going to need to handle will require a specific length of time. For example, when it comes to equipment choices and purchases, you are going to want to do a lot of research before making a decision. You are going to need to find an RV that meets both your physical and financial needs, plus you'll have to decide whether or not you want a tow vehicle and if so what type of vehicle to get.

Start early by attending RV shows and visiting dealerships to get an idea of floor plans, brands, and pricing. Read various online reviews and personal experiences from people around you who may have already tried an RV trip before and take their words with a grain of salt.

As we've already discussed, there is a lot of costs involved in living out of an RV. Costs can include the following:

- Equipment

- Campsite Fees

- Food and Water

- Repairs and Maintenance

- Gas

- Utilities

- Other Personal Expenses

A part of the transition is to determine how you are going to pay for all these categories. Some costs will stay the same, such as your food and gas budget, but depending on the choices you make you make be looking at additional costs for things such as the following:

- Vehicle Loans

- Electricity

- Tools

- Other RV Specific Products

It is my recommendation to save as much money as possible before beginning your transition, for the purpose of not having to scramble at the last minute paying for unexpected fees and bills you did not previously consider. We want to be confident in our budgeting, and even more so in our ability to pay for this chosen lifestyle.

STEP 3: PURCHASE EQUIPMENT

It can take a lot of time and effort to choose an RV that meets your personal and financial preferences. In an upcoming chapter, we are going to look at the types of RV available and help you to see how you can choose the right one for your needs. Take all the time you need for this decision since it is an expensive purchase that can't be undone without hardships.

While we will discuss more about that later, right now just think about three important things that you'll want to start to consider for that chapter:

1. Choose a user-friendly RV with a comfortable floor plan.

2. Choose an RV that meets your lifestyle.

3. Choose a tow vehicle that matches the RV you purchase.

STEP 4: CHOOSE A RESIDENCE

The best thing about an RV is that you are mobile. This means it is easy to move to anyplace you want to go. However, you want to choose your residence carefully. In order to do this, you need to do some research. There are four things you need to consider:

1. Do you want to stay in a campground year-round?

2. Do you want to randomly stay in new places each time?

3. Do you want to buy land and place your RV on it?

4. Do you want to buy a deeded lot in an RV park?

When choosing where you want to stay, you should consider climate, cost of living, location, and safety. Most RV owners prefer to stay in warmer weather climates, but some costs can be higher in these areas. We'll go into greater detail on this at a later point in this book.

STEP 5: DOWNSIZING TO RV LIFE

From a young age, you are raised with the view of holding on to your belongings. Whether it is collecting items as a kid or inheriting antiques or heirlooms from family members, collecting things you'll likely never use again seems to be a general pastime. If you are going to live in an RV, you need to adopt the minimalist lifestyle and reduce the number of all these items you own.

Let's look at what you need to do to have success with the downsizing process.

Downsizing is a major project depending on the size of the house you are coming from and how much you have accumulated over your lifetime. Even a modest home can be about 1,500 square feet, and an average RV can be about 240 square feet. This can be a great challenge, especially if you have emotional attachments to things you've had all your life. Let's get some tips on how you can be successful in the downsizing process.

ORGANIZE FIRST

Rather than attempt to downsize your entire house at one time, view the process as major groups to downsize. You could first start with the smaller items such as trinkets or objects you can sell to an antique shop, donate, or gift. Then move on to clothes, followed by increasingly larger items, saving furniture for the very end.

As you make a decision about which items you want to keep, or which ones you want to store, be mindful of the space available in your RV. The six main groups you'll have to consider include the following:

1. Clothing

2. Kitchen and Household Items

3. Books

4. Files, Papers, and Office Items

5. Tools and Garage Items

6. Furniture

As you focus on each of these groups, make sure you focus on a small area at a time. When you keep your focus on a small section, you can prevent yourself from becoming overwhelmed. You can also make it easier to see progress when working with a small area; this will help keep your motivation up and make it easier to keep going.

As you go through these portions, you should commit to a decision. This means that whenever you pick something up, you should decide: keep it, donate it, or throw it away. Don't set something aside to think about later, since we both know that will never happen. Instead, simply make a decision and stick with it.

CLOTHING

When living in an RV you need to basic casual clothes and in limited quantities. You don't need to pack clothes by the dozens when just three or four shirts and pants are fine. Consider packing some of the following:

☐ Jeans

☐ Lightweight Slacks

☐ Shorts

☐ Shirts

☐ One Dress Outfit

☐ Fleece Jacket or Windbreaker

☐ Raincoat

☐ Sweatshirt or Sweater

☐ Bathing Suit

☐ Knit Cap and Gloves

☐ Woolen Socks and Regular Cotton

☐ Sweatpants

☐ Bathrobe

☐ Pajamas

- ☐ Slippers

- ☐ Hiking Boots

- ☐ Athletic Shoes

- ☐ Dress Shoes

- ☐ Sandals

- ☐ Shower Shoes

Your individual needs will depend on your lifestyle, but oftentimes you are going to have a casual approach for the most part. Be sure to pack the necessities, but keep in mind your available space. After taking a trial run in your RV, pair down your clothes again. It is best to plan to dress in layers rather than packing bulky winter clothing, for instance. Shoes also take up a lot of space so you should limit yourself to only necessary shoes.

Throw away any clothing that is overly worn, torn, or stained. If you see any holes, missing buttons, stretched out elastic or a broken zipper then don't waste your time on it, just throw it away. If clothes are in good condition and you do not have a use for them, you can take them to a donation store if you don't need them in your RV.

There should only be a minimum of sentimental items that you'll store when it comes to clothing such as your wedding dress and suits. My wife actually left her wedding dress for our daughter to keep when the time comes if she ever chooses to get married to whoever makes her happy.

When I asked her how come she didn't keep it stored in our RV, she only looked at me and said, "Well, it's not like I'm going to wear it again anytime soon, now am I?" I laughed and realized she had a very good point.

KITCHEN AND HOUSEHOLD ITEMS

Again, most of these items are going to be based on personal preference and lifestyle. However, to give you some ideas, consider the following useful items when choosing what to keep in your RV:

- ☐ Can Opener

- ☐ Heatproof Silicone Spatulas

- ☐ Wire Whisk

- ☐ Measuring Spoons

- ☐ Measuring Cups

- ☐ Corkscrew

- ☐ Basic Kitchenware (Forks, Knives, Spoons)

- ☐ Drinking Mugs

- ☐ A Serving Spoon

- ☐ Microwave Safe Casserole Dish

- ☐ 13x9 Cake Pan

- ☐ Cookie Sheet

- ☐ Clips to Close Bags

- ☐ Several Sizes of Plastic Storage Containers

- ☐ Plastic Outdoor Tablecloth

- ☐ Dish towels, pot holders, placemats as needed

- ☐ Wooden Spoon

- ☐ Percolator Coffee Pot

- ☐ Small Grill and BBQ Utensils

- ☐ Medium Frying Pan

- ☐ Medium Saucepan

- ☐ Small, Medium, and Large Pots

☐ Aluminum Foil, Plastic Wrap, Zip Lock Bags in Various Sizes

☐ Napkins and Paper Towels

If you have never been too good at baking, you can always omit the cookie sheet or the cake tins and only keep what you do use for cooking regularly. Feel free to modify the list according to your preferences, of course.

Now, an RV is going to have drastically smaller kitchen space than your home, but it can be sufficient if you use that space wisely. Start by choosing the basic kitchen items that you need to have. While going through your item make sure you throw away anything that is any of the following:

- Broken, cracked or chipped

- Worn out

- Frayed, stained, or faded

- Not suitable for donation

Good items to donate include the following:

- Duplicates of items you've already saved.

- Items that are seldom used.

- Items not needed in an RV.

- Items that are too bulky for an RV.

When it comes to household items, you are sure to find some sentimental items that you won't be able to take in the RV. If you can't part with these items, put them in storage or see if there is someone in your family that can hold on to them for you.

FILES, PAPERS, AND OFFICE ITEMS

Papers can accumulate rapidly, and they take up a lot of room. A lot. Of room. Trust me; this is possibly the part I struggled with the most in my downsizing process, due to all the papers we had saved for our However, there are also certain types of papers that you simply can't get rid of for various reasons. Let's consider how you can downsize these items.

Items that should be kept and have paper copies on hand include the following:

- Pet Records - If you are traveling with a pet, then you should keep paper copies proving your pet is free of rabies and has received all the necessary updated vaccines since you'll need to show this at most campgrounds and when crossing the border into Canada or Mexico.

- Insurance - Keep an original paper copy of your insurance policy on hand.

- Identification - You should keep originals of all forms of identification such as driver's license, social security card, and credit cards. You should also keep an electronic form on a flash drive in case you lose any of them.

- Passports and Birth Certificates.

Documents that you can scan and store electronically include the following:

- Financial statements and tax returns.

- Current receipts.

Perhaps one of the more difficult options is old photographs. These are sentimental and can take up a lot of room, or at least a few boxes' worths of albums. If you don't have family that can keep them for you, you could consider scanning them and loading them onto storage cards or digital picture frames while keeping a backup on a cloud service.

If you are going to store any physical photos make sure you take them out of frames and albums to conserve space in your storage shed and keep them in a safe, waterproof container as to avoid any damaging.

Once you have gone through the downsizing process for each area be sure to take a picture of your donation pile before taking it away. This can be a great way to remind yourself of the progress you are making.

You can also have a party and invite family, friends, and colleagues over to take anything from the donation pile, or perhaps hold a garage sale for your neighbors and others who might be interested in a few items or clothes.

Your last option is to consider renting a storage unit if you still have items that you can't part with, but they won't fit in the RV. Just make sure you return to the storage unit at least once a year to go through it and see if there is anything you can get rid of, you may even be able to empty it out at some point. After living on the road for a while, you may find you don't need the items you once thought you did and will be able to part with more of them.

Now that we've gone through the process of transitioning and mentally preparing for life on the road let's get down to the details. Let's start by looking at the RV itself and what you should look for when purchasing your new home.

CHOOSING AND BUYING THE RIGHT RV

There is a lot of research and work that goes into choosing and buying an RV. If you've never traveled in an RV, this can be an even more difficult process.

The first step involved is to research the types of RV there currently are and learn how everything in an RV works, so you have a good idea of what model is right for you. Then it is a matter of looking around and finding the right one that fits your particular needs and making the final purchase.

CLASSES OF RV

Class A and C Motorhomes   Fifth Wheels   Toy Haulers

Van Campers and Class Bs   Travel Trailers   Hybrids

The first step you want to take in researching and choosing your RV is to learn about the classes of RVs. You've likely heard people talking about RVs and may be slightly confused about what it all means. Or perhaps you've been looking at pictures of RVs and don't know what class they are or how to tell if they would be a good fit for you. So let's get an overview of your options.

First, RVs are separated into two broad categories before being broken down into further options. There are towable rigs and motor coaches.

As the name suggests, towable rigs require a tow vehicle, and it typically needs to be a powerful one. For your larger trailers and fifth wheels, you'll likely need at least a half-ton and possibly a one-ton truck to tow safely.

Even smaller travel trailers may at least require a large SUV to pull them. There are some ultra-lightweight trailers that can be pulled behind smaller vehicles and even some cars. While these trailers are cheaper, you should also take into consideration the cost of the tow vehicle when making a purchase decision.

FOLDING CAMPING TRAILERS

Also known as pop-ups, these are lightweight units with sides that collapse for towing and storage. They give you open-air tent camping along with a comfortable sleeping area, basic amenities, and protection from the weather. They can be 15 to 23 feet when opened and cost around $4,000 to $12,000 depending on your desired floor plan. They can keep up to eight people. The benefits of these trailers are the following:

☐ Good for first time RV owners due to the low price.

☐ Allows towing by most vehicles and easy to maneuver into tight spaces by hand.

☐ Quick to set up and provides basic spaces when setting up.

☐ Some models can come with modern amenities such as stoves, refrigerators, and showers.

These are loaded on and attached to the bed of a pickup. They are good for back road travel since they can access more remote locations, and can be between 18 to 21 feet. Prices range from $4,000 to $22,000 with the truck sold separately. Depending on the model you choose they can house up to six people. The benefits of these trailers are the following:

☐ An economical option for those who already have a pickup truck.

☐ Offers the best of both stand-alone motorhomes and towable trailers.

☐ You have the option of detaching and setting up on jacks so you can use the truck independently.

☐ There is a wide range of floor plans, including ones with a toilet, showers, kitchen, pop-up roofs, and air conditioning.

TRAVEL TRAILERS

These units are designed to be towed by another vehicle using a bumper or frame hitch and are great for full-time living. They can range in size from 12 to 35 feet long. The cost lies between $9,000 and $63,000 depending on the floor plan and amenities you choose. They can typically sleep up to eight people. The benefits of travel trailers are the following:

☐ Can be detached from the tow vehicle so the tow vehicle can be used for errands and short trips.

☐ Offers you all the conveniences of a home and come with a wide range of floor plans to meet your individual needs.

☐ Most models offer a slide out to give you more living space.

FIFTH WHEEL TRAILERS

These are designed to be towed by a pickup truck with a special hitch in the truck bed, and they offer the best experience of all towable units. They can be 21 to 40 feet in length, and cost an average of $13,000 to $97,000. Depending on the floor plan they can sleep up to eight people. The benefits of these trailers are the following:

☐ Can be detached from the tow vehicle so the tow vehicle can be used for short trips and errands.

☐ Slide outs offer increased living space.

☐ Newer lightweight fifth wheels can be towed by smaller trucks.

The main drawback to these units is the fact that most fifth wheels require properly equipped and compatible pickups. The weight of the trailer needs to be matched with a vehicle of the correct towing capacity.

TOY HAULERS

Toy haulers are available in both towable and motorized formats. They are basically home with a garage attached. In the garage area, you can take some toys with you whether it be an ATV or another small vehicle.

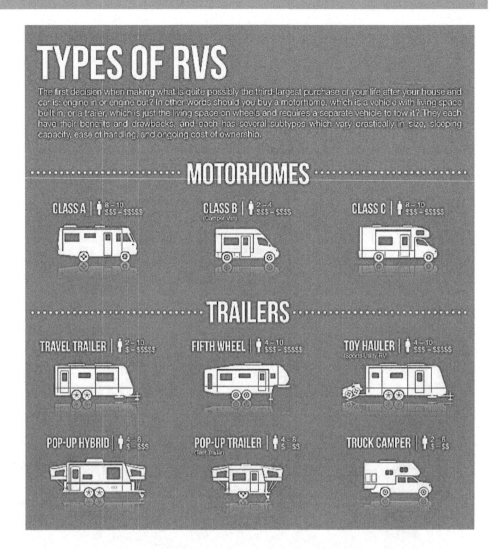

TYPES OF RVS

The first decision when making what is quite possibly the third-largest purchase of your life after your house and car is: engine in or engine out? In other words should you buy a motorhome, which is a vehicle with living space built in, or a trailer, which is just the living space on wheels and requires a separate vehicle to tow it? They each have their benefits and drawbacks, and each has several subtypes which vary drastically in size, sleeping capacity, ease of handling, and ongoing cost of ownership.

MOTORHOMES

CLASS A | 8 – 10 | $$$ – $$$$$

CLASS B (Camper Van) | 2 – 4 | $$$ – $$$$

CLASS C | 8 – 10 | $$$ – $$$$$

TRAILERS

TRAVEL TRAILER | 2 – 10 | $ – $$$$$

FIFTH WHEEL | 4 – 10 | $$$ – $$$$$

TOY HAULER (Sports Utility RV) | 4 – 10 | $$$ – $$$$$

POP-UP HYBRID | 4 – 8 | $ – $$$

POP-UP TRAILER (Tent Trailer) | 4 – 8 | $ – $$

TRUCK CAMPER | 2 – 6 | $ – $$

Now that we have discussed the types of towable vehicles let's look at motor coaches. These are self-powered RVs with their own engine and driving chassis. The difference between these and towable trailers is the camping experience. With a towable trailer, you can't enjoy the amenities until you have finished your drive and set up the trailer. In some places, an oversized towable RV may not be allowed without extra license requirements.

On the other hand, a motor coach allows you to simply stop at a camping spot with no need to set up the unit. The drawback is that you will have a harder time getting around locally unless you tow a smaller vehicle behind your RV. Let's look more closely at the different types of motor coaches to choose from.

CLASS A MOTOR COACH

The largest and most amenity-filled option when it comes to RVs. They are truly a home on wheels. They are a fully loaded bus perfect for full-time living. They can be 21 to 40 feet long with an average cost of $50,000 to $500,000. Depending on your floor plan, they can sleep up to ten people. These units come with the following benefits:

☐ The units are spacious and often come with luxury amenities such as basement storage, washer/dryers, hydraulic leveling, and security systems, and sometimes even hot tubs.

☐ Some units come with slide outs to increase living space.

☐ They typically offer a smooth and steady drive, so they work well for long distance travel with no special license required.

☐ Everything is accessible in these units.

☐ You have the option of towing a small vehicle for use once you stop at your destination.

CLASS B MOTOR COACH

Also known as a camper van, these are typically cargo vans that are customized for temporary sleeping, eating, and bathroom facilities. These units can be from 16 to 21 feet and cost from $35,000 to $65,000. Depending on the floor plan they can sleep up to four people. These units have the following benefits:

☐ This is your most money-friendly RV and can even be used as a second vehicle.

☐ They are versatile and easy to maneuver.

☐ The van body means they are often narrower than an RV but are still ideal for couples.

CLASS C MOTOR COACH

Also called a mini-motorhome. These units offer all the convenience of a larger RV, but with a smaller size and associated price tag. They are an automotive van frame with an attached cab. They can be between 20 to 28 feet long and cost about $45,000 to $75,000. Depending on your floor plan they can sleep up to six people. These units have the following benefits:

- ☐ They typically have a sleeping bunk over the cab area, which can also be used for storage.

- ☐ While they are smaller than a Class A, they still provide appropriate space and privacy for relaxed living.

- ☐ Some units come with a slide out for increased living space.

These are the main types of RVs to choose from. Once you have an idea of which RV is best for you, take the time to look at a few in real life and get a feel for them. If needed, rent one for a trip to make sure you can live in it full-time before making a decision. Another thing you'll want to research and learn before you start shopping is to learn how everything works in an RV.

HOW EVERYTHING WORKS IN AN RV

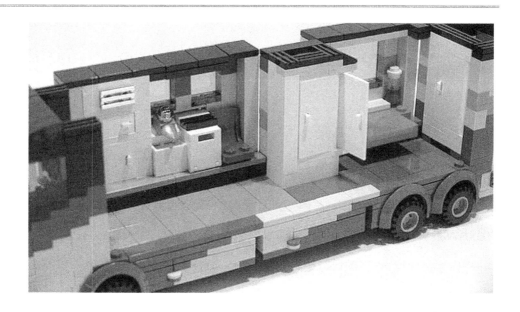

When you go to an RV dealer, they will likely give you a tour of the RV and show you all the functions and features. Even if you don't know the ins and outs of an RV at this time, it is important that you get to know how everything works in an RV at some point since you are going to be the one operating and maintaining them.

In this chapter, I'm going to cover all the basics of RVs. I promise there will be no technical diagrams and high-level engineering; I'm only going to tell you what you need to know in order to familiarize yourself with all the main systems on an RV.

THE WATER SYSTEMS

This is perhaps one of the most important resources when you are living on the road. Whether you are boondocking or staying at an RV resort, you are going to need to find access to water.

FRESHWATER TANKS VERSUS CITY HOOKUPS

HOW THE FRESHWATER TANK WORKS

There are two ways that you can add water to your RV water system. The first is to literally add water to your freshwater tank. This is typically a 10 to 30-gallon tank that allows you to store water. The spot where you fill up this tank is often clearly marked. You can fill up this tank with a hose, which this can be done at most big freeway gas stations, parks, campgrounds, and even a few cities.

If for any reason you don't have access to a free water source then you can buy some portable five to six-gallon water jugs to fill up your freshwater tank. About the only place where you can fill up your jugs is in dispersed camping locations such as BLM lands and occasionally parks that don't have water sources available.

WATER PUMPS

Once you have filled your freshwater tank, you may find nothing happens when you turn on a faucet. Even if you have water in your tank, it doesn't mean there is pressure–this is why RVs have a water pump. There will be a switch labeled "water pump," and you need to turn it on every time you want to use the water.

It is important to note that the water pump runs off your RVs battery, or the 12-volt system I'll talk about soon. The water pump is best used when boondocking since you can otherwise use a city water hookups with built-in water pressure and save the remaining water for another more urgent occasion.

There should always be a filter installed between the freshwater tank and the pump. This will ensure dust and debris don't get inside the pump, since any of it could ruin the entire system. If you turn on the pump and nothing happens, you most likely have an issue with your water pump involving the filter malfunctioning.

CONSERVING FRESHWATER

You want to consider the conservation of your freshwater. In a typical house with a family of four, the average water use is 400 gallons a day. There is no RV that can hold anywhere close to this so you'll need to practice freshwater conservation. There are several easy ways to do achieve that goal.

1. Don't run the water while brushing your teeth or showering. Some people already have a designated cup of water they reserve for when they brush their teeth, so they avoid running water altogether unless it is to refill the cup.

2. Learn how to take six-minute showers at a time.

3. Drink bottled water. Now, there are a few restaurants that have a policy of giving free complimentary water to their customers or to anyone who arrives in their establishment. With the proper research and occasionally purchasing small items at a time, it is possible to acquire the majority of your drinking water free of charge elsewhere.

4. Find new ways to wash dishes and avoid using products like dishwashers and washing machines. You could wash them by hand immediately after using them, so the pieces of food do not stick, making the process much longer. Alternatively, you could also reuse your plates if they did not encounter particularly messy foods. Disposable plates are also an option but are a bit more complicated for those who love to cook.

5. If possible, install low flow faucets and showerheads.

Thankfully most RVs are designed to use less water so that they will help you throughout this process. Come to think about it, these rules are also pretty valid if you are living in a house, as saving and conserving water has become a lot more important throughout the years and is something we ought to practice more often.

CITY WATER CONNECTIONS

While this is called city water connections, it can actually refer to any time you are directly hooking up to a faucet that is directly connected to a water source. This is often a water hookup at an RV park, for example, and consists of the simple process of screwing one end of the hose into your rig and the other into the spigot at your site. Once connected, you simply turn the spigot, and you have water.

There are a few other things to consider with this option. The primary thing to consider is water pressure. In older RVs, the plumbing isn't designed to withstand the water pressure of most water sources. If you have too much pressure it can break your pipes, cause leaky joints, or dripping faucets.

It is well worth your time to consider purchasing a water pressure regulator; this small metal cylinder is worth your money if you are going to be staying at a lot of places with water hookups. This will typically need to be replaced once a year, so you are good to go until those 365 days.

WATER FILTERS

A water filter is just as important as the filter for your water pump. However, it is less about keeping out debris and more about filtering out impurities in the water system so you can be sure you are drinking safe, potable water. Water filters are often attached to the end of the hose furthest away from the RV.

One question you'll likely have when you start RV living is, what is the difference between gray water and black water? The answer can be simple depending on what you want to know. Blackwater is essentially human waste and what you put down the toilet. Greywater is what goes down the shower, kitchen, and bathroom sink.

In some states or areas, particularly Southwestern states, you are often allowed to drop greywater onto the ground. It is always best to ask a park manager or ranger for information on where and how to dump so you don't get in trouble.

Although in general, you don't want to dump gray water near a freshwater source like a lake or creek, since the watershed can serve many people and animals. Blackwater, on the other hand, needs to be dumped in a sewage system as mandated by law.

THE SEWAGE SYSTEM

While the sewage system is essentially an extension of the water system, there are a few things that are specifically related to the sewage system and disposal that you need to understand. Most of it is related to keeping the system from getting clogged. We'll discuss the process of cleaning and emptying later.

It is important to know that the RV sewage system can easily become clogged. The best thing you can do is use special toilet paper for RVs. Another option is to use it for bowel movements as little as possible and when you do, to have as much water in there as possible. When you have a lot of water in the tank, then it will help break up any solid waste.

It can also be a good idea to fill the tank before your next drive so the sloshing will help crush everything so it can be easier to clean out when you dump. I know it does not sound like a very appealing subject, but it is better for us to cover it here than for you to try to learn about it in a rather unpleasant way later on.

Another option is to purchase the small packets of bacteria that can be flushed down the toilet to help break up solid material. However, they have a mixture of reviews, so it is up to you if you want to try using these.

ELECTRICAL SYSTEMS

Most RVs have two basic electrical systems: the 120-volt and the 12-volt, or 120v and 12v. The 120v is similar to what is in a standard home with the typical electrical outlets. The 12v is similar to what you have in a vehicle, such as the cigarette adapters.

When you are plugged into an RV hookup, you'll typically use the 120v system, and you'll be able to use anything such as the air conditioner, fans, microwaves, any necessary electronic equipment. When you are plugged into an RV connection, the 120v system will charge the 12v system.

If you are boondocking and don't have an external power source, then you'll need to use your 12v system. Most RVs have a refrigerator that runs off a 12v, and the lights will work, but not much else will work. Some newer RVs will have a converter that allows your computer and other low-intensity devices to charge them, but the power won't last long without a renewable energy source like solar panels or a generator.

The 12v system won't have enough power for higher intensity electronics such as the air conditioner, microwaves, or hair dryers

When plugging into an RV park power source, there will typically be three types of amperage: 20, 30 and 50. A 20 amp outlet looks like your normal wall outlet. A 30 amp outlet has one circular hole at the bottom and two parallel slots angled inward near the top. 50 amp plugs have a different structure.

You can purchase adapters, but it isn't ideal to go up in amps. Most RVs are designed for either 30 or 50 amp, and most RV parks offer both.

WATTS, AMPS, AND VOLTS

If you don't do a lot of electrical work, you may find the terminology complicated. Amps are the energy you use or the actual amount of electricity. Volts are the power of energy. Watts are what you can accomplish with the amount and power available to you.

GENERATORS

A generator can help you keep your 12v battery charged by just running it a little in the morning and a little in the evening. However, many are switching to the solar option since a generator requires you to store gas, they are noisy, and they create pollution although it is a good idea to have a generator on hand even if you have solar since it isn't always sunny.

BREAKER BOX VERSUS 12V FUSE BOX

RVs have electrical boxes that are the same as the ones in your house. They work just the same too. They switch to prevent overloads. Knowing where it is located is very important since fuses are one of the biggest things that can go wrong. They are easy to switch out if you have issues, of course, but you always want to be particularly careful to not accidentally start a fire or go as far as to electrocute yourself.

PROPANE

Propane plays important roles in your RV including keeping your refrigerator cold, your water hot, and even meets some electrical needs. There are three ways that you can get propane on board your RV.

EXCHANGEABLE CYLINDERS

Many towable trailers come with a spot near the hitch where you can store and hook up propane tanks. Even those who haven't been in an RV yet know what a propane tank looks like. Exchangeable cylinders can cost more than simply getting your own tanks filled. If you are going with this option, you should at least have two tanks since the tank will need to be completely empty before you can exchange it.

PORTABLE, REMOVABLE, REFILLABLE TANKS

This is often the best choice. While the tanks are expensive, you can buy larger tanks of 30 to 40 pounds that don't need to be refilled as often. The only drawback is that it can be difficult to find a place that will refill propane, and when you do, it can be a time-consuming process. However, financially-speaking it may be worth the effort if you play your cards right.

PERMANENT TANKS

The main drawback with this option is it can be harder to get the permanent tanks recertified, and you can't detach them from the RV. This means you have to take the RV with you when you need to refill them and this can be inconvenient and difficult, particularly when you have back pains.

KITCHEN APPLIANCES

REFRIGERATORS

RV refrigerators typically come as two kinds: two and three-way. A two-way fridge can run off propane and requires you to be connected to the 12v battery, but can also run off 30 amp power if you are plugged into a park hookup. A three-way refrigerator does all of the above, but can also run off the RV batteries on its own. These refrigerators also tend to be larger and hold more food.

STOVE AND OVEN

Most stoves you find in an RV don't vary much from the standard gas stove in your home. The only difference is they are often smaller, so you will just have to adapt to that in your own way.

SINKS

The main thing differentiating the sinks in an RV over the ones in your home is the pipes and holding tanks. If any food waste goes down your sink drain, it can quickly clog the pipes.

It is also important that you fix any leaks right away to reduce water waste and to prevent moisture buildup in your RV. So, just make sure all your dishes no longer have food on them when you set them in the sink for a wash, and that you do not toss any solid items down the pipes.

JACKS AND LEVELING

There are many reasons why you want your RV to stay level, but the main reason is your refrigerator. If a refrigerator is running on propane, then it needs to be leveled. Otherwise, an airlock can develop, and that can be very difficult to fix.

We'll discuss more about the leveling system and how to level an RV later, but here I just want to remind you that it is best to choose a system in the middle. You don't want an entirely electric system, but you don't want a hand crank system that is prone to failing easily.

HEATERS

Even if you are staying in warmer climates, it can still get cold at night. Or perhaps you are traveling in colder weather to avoid the larger crowds that visit in warmer weather. There are three ways that you can add heat to your RV.

SPACE HEATERS

The typical space heaters you use in your home are a cheap way to heat your RV, but you will need at least a 20 amp service. Space heaters are good for short term use when boondocking or while using the generator.

CATALYTIC HEATERS

These are an excellent choice since they can heat your RV without electricity and less propane than a built-in propane heater. However, the dangers of using these are a little higher and aren't recommended if you are traveling with pets or kids in the RV. It is best to make sure you have fresh air coming in also when using these heaters so you can avoid any accidental injuries.

BUILT-IN PROPANE HEATERS

These, in general, aren't the best option for a few reasons. First, they use more propane than the catalytic heaters, and they need electricity since they use a fan to blow heat into the RV interior. So unless you plan always to be hooked up to a power supply at an RV park, these generally aren't a great option. If you do use one, be prepared to burn through your propane pretty fast.

Now that you know the ins and outs of an RV, it is time to start considering what type of RV is right for you. You've probably been looking at magazines and websites, so you have a visual on a type of RV you like. But what else do you need to consider when choosing an RV? Let's take a look.

WHAT TO CONSIDER WHEN CHOOSING AN RV

Even if your reason for purchasing an RV is to retire and live in it full-time, there are still a range of goals and purposes for why people are going to make this particular move. No matter what your reason may be, you need to be careful in choosing an RV because no two RVs are the same, and you need to make the right choice in order to be happy and comfortable with your new lifestyle.

The first thing to do is realize that you'll never find the perfect RV, but you can come close. This means you'll have to make some compromises when choosing your vehicle. It is best to come up with a list of things you want in an RV and adapt as you research and prepare for life on the road, so it is easier to find the right one when you start shopping around for a unit.

Let's look at what you have to consider when choosing an RV.

CONSTRUCTION

For someone living full-time in an RV, the construction is more important than someone getting an RV for casual traveling. This is because year-round RV living puts a lot of wear and tear on the unit. Therefore, look for sturdy furniture made from materials that will last.

Cabinets should be made from solid types of wood and metal and quality latches since they will be opened and closed constantly. Solid flooring such as ceramic tile is easier to clean and can last the life of the unit if properly maintained.

An aluminum roof that is solid and overlaps the front and rear of the unit will be less likely to leak than other roofs. Aluminum sides with full body paint are going to look better than most units and will last longer as well. You should have dual pane windows since these will balance the climate inside and lower noise levels coming in from the outside.

DESIGN

There is no shortage of design configurations for RVs, so you want to make sure you choose a floor plan that is going to be comfortable for you without being too small or too unnecessarily large if there will only be two people living there. Look for the following when checking out the interior of an RV:

- No overstuffed furniture.

- Large windows.

- Pass through bathrooms.

- Island beds.

- Kitchen space.

- Well-designed storage areas.

- Blinds instead of curtains.

- Slide rooms.

SIZE

Length is often one of the biggest issues for people when choosing an RV. While a larger unit could provide a more comfortable living environment, it can also be more difficult to drive and maneuver in small cities. On the other hand, a smaller unit may not be the best for a comfortable full-time living environment if both parties of travelers struggle with claustrophobia or cramped spaces. Choosing the right length can be difficult.

Keep in mind that when living in an RV you are going to be in it the majority of the time. However, if you aren't able to get it from one destination to the other, then there really isn't much point to having an RV in the first place.

Thankfully, slide rooms have solved part of that problem since they provide extra room and a smaller RV for easier travel. However, you also want to be careful when it comes to slide-outs in general. If you have too many or too large of a slide-out, then you won't be able to simply stop and take a break without setting up your full RV.

For someone who wants to travel a lot, a unit with extra-slide outs may not be the best option.

TYPE

Most people choose to live full-time in trailers, fifth wheels, or motor homes. Oftentimes, people won't choose van conversions or campers. Each type comes with their pros and cons, so study each design and type carefully before making a decision. Just remember to consider the type of RV along with the driving ability when making a choice.

Perhaps one of the biggest factors influencing a decision is the cost. Whether this is the cost of the unit itself or the cost of traveling and living, you want to find something that can fit within your budget as well. This is why it is important to take your time and go to RV shows and dealerships to see what is available and find a unit that is affordable for your budget.

It is often a good idea to consider an older unit rather than a newer one since they are more reliable and already have long-standing reviews from previous users. You may also be able to find a better deal on an older unit since there are new models that are more expensive coming out every so often.

Also, keep in mind that things will change and what may work at one time won't always work in the context of every trip you have in mind. So if you can, consider purchasing a used, reliable RV at first so you can budget and change as needed to adapt to full-time RV living.

Keeping all of this in mind, I want to give you my five top picks for units that work for a more permanent arrangement. This doesn't mean you need to buy one of these five, but it can at least give you an idea of what you are looking for.

TOP FIVE RVS FOR FULL-TIME LIVING

To help you get started making a decision on the right RV for your needs, consider the top five RVs for full-time living and see what you may want in your own vehicle.

#1 - COACHMEN CHAPARRAL FIFTH WHEEL

This is the ultimate machine in luxury living with its 11 different floor plans to choose from. It weighs 9,575 to 12,694 pounds unloaded and ranges from 33 to 41 feet in length. It can sleep four to eleven people. The number of floor plans makes this one of the more flexible options, and for a luxury RV, it is a little on the lighter side, making it easier to tow.

It also offers numerous storage options and electronic upgrades with plenty more upgrade features to choose from. In other words, you will be able to design your vehicle based on your own custom preferences and needs.

#2 - JAYCO NORTH POINT FIFTH WHEEL

This is your heavy duty option for backwoods living. There are nine-floor plan options to choose from. Unloaded it can weigh between 12,405 and 14,200 pounds. Length can range from 38 to 43 feet and sleeps four to nine people. Although bulky and heavy, this RV is stable and very durable for rugged use. It comes with an insulated underbelly so that you can stay comfortable in any climate. It can also support an outdoor kitchen for a truly wonderful camping experience if you are a fan of cooking.

A smaller yet equally as comfortable option. There are 11-floor plans to choose from. Unloaded weight can be 8,307 to 12,896 pounds. They vary from 30 to 42 feet in length and can sleep two to nine people. This is an excellent option for couples since it offers a decent length with a lightweight for easy travel.

It also offers some impressive features, including three slide-outs in each floorplan to give you plenty of ample space for visits. It also offers a residential style refrigerator with plenty of room for any foods you desire.

An affordable option for families. This one has ten-floor plans to choose from. Unloaded, it weighs 10,605 to 12,300 pounds. It can be 36 to 42 feet in length depending on the model and can sleep four to ten people. This is your best option if you have a tight budget since it offers excellent features and versatility for a price lower than similar RVs.

The RV comes with a default luxury package, but can also have more features added with expansions and optimizations.

General all-around well-built fifth wheel. It offers impressive 23-floor plans to choose from. Unloaded it can weigh 7,466 to 13,170 pounds. Depending on the model it can be 31 to 42 feet long and sleep four to ten people. This is perhaps your lightest and most spacious option. It also has quite a satisfying amount of features to choose from based on your desired upgrades.

Now that you are sure to have narrowed your choices let's look into what you should actually do when purchasing one.

FIVE THINGS TO CONSIDER
BEFORE BUYING AN RV

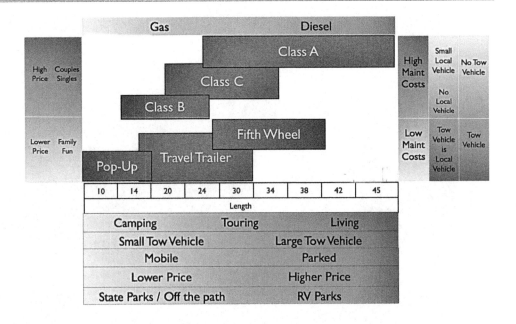

Before you head out to purchase your first RV, or should I say your new home, there are five things you should do first.

VISIT RV DEALERSHIPS

Take the time to visit various RV dealerships just to look at what is out there and talk to the salespeople about tips, recommendations, and information on the brands. Walk around units and get a feel for the layouts, brands, and lengths. Reading about the units won't give you the same feel as actually walking through a unit and seeing the sizes in the case for yourself.

DEVELOP A WISH LIST

One thing that will help you when shopping is to put together a wish list, the same as when you looked for and bought your home. Be specific and picky in your wish list, since this is your chance to dream. From this list, you can use the options you write down to narrow everything down to the items that are must-haves.

Consider things that are necessary to maintain a happy lifestyle over those that are just cosmetic details, or that will not actually affect you if they are included or not. Some factors you may want to have on the list are:

- Cost

- All seasons unit

- At least one slide out

- Lots of storage

- Weight if towing the unit

CONSIDER USED RVS

It is often a good idea to purchase a used unit rather than a new one. RVs will lose value quickly and buying a brand new vehicle doesn't necessarily mean fewer problems. In fact, people tend to have more problems with upcoming units.

It often takes a few years for a unit to work out its issues, or for those issues to even present themselves. Plus, you may be able to buy a unit from someone who has only used it once or twice and is now looking to sell because it didn't fit their lifestyle, or they only wanted a unit for a determined period of time that has now ended. This can be a great way to save some money.

Just make sure you are careful in picking a used RV by ensuring it meets the criteria we will discuss shortly.

KNOW HOW YOU'LL USE YOUR RV

When choosing an RV, it is highly important to pick on that meets your lifestyle, as we have covered before. For example, if you want to adventure travel and boondock often then you may want a more durable unit. On the other hand, if you want to travel in RV parks and cities, you will want a small and more maneuverable unit.

Depending on how you like to spend your days, it may vary the type of amenities you want to look for. How much time you spend in boondocking versus at parks will influence the type of hookups you have and additions you'll need, like solar panels.

DON'T OVEREXTEND

It is important that you set a budget early on and stick to it. It is easy to get away from your budget when it comes to choosing upgrades and amenities, which is why you must keep in mind an objective perspective of what you really need. Going for the more luxurious, large option may sound like a great idea on paper, but in practice could be more difficult to maintain and handle than a smaller, equally as a comfortable unit that includes a more basic set-up.

Keep in mind what is really important and remember you can always make small cosmetic changes down the line when you have a little money set aside and truly know what amenities and upgrades you need. For example, you technically do not need a hot tub included in your RV, or a fully equipped kitchen with an oven if neither you nor your travel partner intend to bake dishes very often.

Because it can quickly become a chore or a more sour type of activity, remember to keep the purchase process fun and keep sight of the benefits to come when living from your RV. Once you've finally settled on an RV you want, there are a few things you want to check before making the final deal and signing any dotted lines for an official transaction.

WHAT TO CHECK WHEN BUYING AN RV

Once you've settled on an RV and are ready to make a purchase there are a few things you want to test and check beforehand. This is especially important if you haven't spent much time in an RV. Most dealers will offer you a complete walkthrough, but it is up to you to check out the systems thoroughly and to ask the right questions.

It is important that you don't buy an RV without testing everything, which also means testing everything in the hooked-up mode as well as boondocking mode. To do this, make sure you bring the following with you:

☐ Water Hose

☐ Charged Car or Marine Battery

☐ Cigarette Lighter Power Adapter

☐ 30 or 50 amp to Normal Outlet Adapter

☐ Phone and Standard Wall Charger

☐ 20-pound Propane Cylinder

TESTING THE WATER SYSTEM

Start by hooking a hose up, one to the water intake line and the other to a source of running water. Once water is flowing into the RV, you should go inside and turn on all faucets and flush the toilet. Water pressure should be equal to what your hose is hooked up to. Leave the water flowing for a few minutes while you look underneath for any signs of leaks.

If you have access to a drain, hook up the sewer hose and test it. Even if you don't have access to a drain you should be able to do it in the yard since there won't be any black water in the unit. Make sure everything drains from both grey and black water tanks with no leaking.

Back inside, look under the sink and in the bathroom to see what type of plumbing is installed. Then fill up the freshwater storage. Turn on the water pump and ensure it sounds like it is running appropriately. Again, test the faucets inside and ensure everything is working appropriately. If everything is working fine and there are no leaks, you are good for the water system.

TESTING THE ELECTRICAL SYSTEM

As we've already discussed, most RVs can run directly off a 12v battery or plug into a power source at an RV park, whether it be 50 or 30 amp. Often, there is a fuse box for the 12v aspect that runs off the battery and a breaker box similar to the one at your house that controls 120v appliances.

Most lights and internal indicators are powered by 12v. Some refrigerators can run on 12v as well, or it can run on propane when not plugged into an outlet. Air conditioners and wall outlets will run on 120v, and this won't usually be an option when boondocking in your RV.

To test the 12v system, make sure a good battery is connected to the RV then head inside to turn on some lights. If you have the correct adapter with you, test out the cigarette lighter 12v outlets. Also, check fuses to make sure they are all good and double check the battery to ensure there is power.

Once all this checks out, you can plug the external power cable into an electric source. You should bring an adapter to plug into a normal wall outlet. Go back inside and make sure all the power sources are working. Plug your phone into outlets to easily test them. Turn on the air conditioning to make sure it is working. If everything is up to speed, then you can move to the next system.

TESTING THE PROPANE SYSTEM

The last major system you want to check is the propane system. Propane is going to fuel your stove, water heater, and potentially other heaters and backup your refrigerator as well. Hook up a propane tank and open the line to hear a hiss as propane enters the lines of the RV.

Head inside and turn on the stove and then light a match. The burner should light in about two minutes, maximum. You will have to light a pilot light in the oven to test it. Unplug the outside power cable if it is still plugged in and if needed adjust the control panel to the appropriate setting. Ensure the refrigerator continues to run on propane. Since it can sometimes take hours for the refrigerator to get cold, you may want to ask the seller to turn it on in advance of your arrival.

Lastly, find access to the water heater and follow instructions to light it. You'll often be able to see and hear it working. Within about 20 minutes you should be able to feel warm water in the RV by turning a faucet to hot.

These are the main systems you want to try out and ensure they are working. However, there may be some additional systems you want to check out to make sure they are to your liking and comfort.

OTHER THINGS TO CHECK

If there is access to a television and cable outlet, you can test the cable connection and the entertainment systems. Test any fans and windows to ensure they open and are easy to operate. Lastly, take the RV for a test drive to ensure you are comfortable driving it.

INSPECTING A USED RV

If you choose to buy a used RV, you'll want to check the above, plus a few extra things.

The roof is difficult to examine but should be checked on any used RV. If there are issues with the roof and you don't discover it before purchase, it can easily cost you thousands of dollars to replace. Find out what material the roof is made out of and then climb up and take a look, or have a trustworthy more agile person up there if you are otherwise unable to do it yourself.

If the roof is vinyl, blisters and bubbles can develop when exposed to the sun for long periods of time, and leaks can result from that.

Metal roofs need recoating along the seams annually. As long as the wood under the metal is undamaged, the roof can be cheaper to replace and maintain as needed.

In addition to the roof itself, you should also locate all the vents and A/C unit and look for water stains or other discoloration. Look at the ceiling inside where the wall meets for discoloration. It can also be a good idea to look in cabinets and closets as well.

THE FLOOR

Even if the roof is in good condition, you should also check the floor for signs of water damage. In the winter months, unused RVs can have the pipes freeze and leak. Any plumbing leaks tend to go unnoticed until it is used for camping again. Most RV floors are made from particle board, which will deteriorate if exposed to moisture for long periods of time.

Closely look at the floor in the kitchen and bathrooms. Tap the floor with a blunt object to see if the wood is soft in any places. Check under the cabinets for any sign of flooding or discoloration along the floor and walls.

Floor repairs can be expensive especially if you have to replace joists. The floor covering itself often isn't that expensive to be replaced and may be done if you want to update your flooring.

BRAKES, TIRES, AND LEVELING SYSTEMS

All RVs use tires and brakes the same as any other vehicle. While the cost of tires is similar to vehicles, some types can be more expensive. If the tires look worn or weather-cracked, it is best to take note of the tire size and check out the cost for replacement before purchasing.

Drive or pull the unit in order to look at the brakes. A brake repair isn't cheap for an RV and brakes are essential safety devices, so it is crucial you don't ignore this step. If the brakes take too long to respond or are a bit rusted, it is best for you to compare the costs of repairing them rather than to face the consequences of an accident later on.

So now we have all you need to look for, let's take a look at a checklist you can use when going out to buy your RV.

RV BUYING CHECKLIST (EXTERIOR & INTERIOR)

When you go to buy an RV, it can be a good idea to have a checklist with you to ensure you don't forget to check something. Consider the following checklist to help you.

Exterior

☐ No rust on the bottom of the chassis.

☐ Clean and dry roof with no cracks or peeling.

☐ Clean engine and generator compartments.

☐ No signs of corrosion, oil leaks, or rust in the engine and generator compartments.

- ☐ No fogging on windows.

- ☐ Jacks move smoothly.

- ☐ TV antennas move smoothly.

- ☐ Steps work well.

- ☐ No scrapes, dents, bubbling, faded paint or peeling on the body.

- ☐ No worn or cracked tires.

- ☐ No leaking on slide rooms.

- ☐ Slide rooms work smoothly and easily.

Interior

- ☐ No windshield cracks.

- ☐ Slide rooms function well and sit properly.

- ☐ Passenger seat reclines properly.

- ☐ Windows open and close easily.

- ☐ No rust or missing parts on light fixtures.

- ☐ Ceiling vent fans work.

- [ ] Digital televisions and antennas.

- [ ] No damaged or stained flooring.

- [ ] No air conditioner leaks.

- [ ] No leaking faucets.

- [ ] No signs of water damage, especially in closets and cabinets.

- [ ] Cabinet doors and drawers open easily and shut completely.

- [ ] Wood is of good quality and not mismatched.

- [ ] No ammonia odor in the refrigerator.

- [ ] The ice maker is present.

- [ ] No rust or dirt under the stove burner.

- [ ] No burns, cracks, or scratches on countertops.

- [ ] No worn or damaged upholstery.

- [ ] No unpleasant odors.

- [ ] No propane odors.

- [ ] No mildew smell.

☐ No sewer tank odor.

11 RED FLAGS WHEN BUYING AN RV

After all this, you are going to find a decent RV, but if you are planning to buy a used one, you are likely to find some type of problem unless it comes from a reliable source. Some of these problems aren't that bad and can be fixed with no further complications.

However, there are 11 red flags that you need to look out for as indications you should never buy an RV if any of those flags are found. Let's look at them in detail.

#1 - Delamination

Delamination occurs for one of two reasons:

1. The glue connecting the outer walls to the inner walls has dried out or lost strength.

2. Water has seeped into the seams, and external walls have loosened in areas.

The problem isn't difficult to fix, but can be expensive. Look for bubbling or indentations. Even just one or two small areas should be a red flag to avoid purchasing the RV.

#2 - Rubber Roof

The best RVs have roofs made of aluminum or fiberglass. If the unit you are considering has a rubber roof, then you are going to be making a costly mistake. Rubber roofs aren't durable and both difficult and expensive to repair. Sometimes replacement can cost as much as $8,000.

#3 - Old Tires

If tires are over five-years-old, then you should either negotiate the price with the seller or pass on purchasing the RV altogether. Old tires aren't safe to use and replacing them with good quality RV tires is a costly expense.

#4 - Signs of Water Damage

Water leaks are common in RVs, but if they aren't fixed right away, they can cause structural damage. If there is any sign of water leaks on the ceiling, along with slide areas or inside cabinets, then you may want to pass on the RV. It could have hidden and extensive damage. Pass on anything with visible signs of damage or mildew smell.

#5 - Clogged A/C Filter

If the A/C filter is dirty, this can be a sign that the RV hasn't been maintained properly. This means other regular maintenance may not have been done. If other areas of the RV aren't clean either, you should pass on the unit.

#6 - Cigarette Smell

RVs tend to pick up odors easily, and some can be eliminated easily while others are difficult to remove. Cigarette smell is one that is hard to remove unless you completely overhaul the interior. For a smoker, this may not matter; but for a non-smoker, this might be a hard pass.

#7 - Pet Odors

If you don't own pets or if you are allergic to them, buying a used RV that had pets at some point can be uncomfortable. It can be difficult to remove pet odor smell and hair. Unless you are okay with deep cleaning the interior, you may want to pass on these units.

#8 - Sewer Smell

Blackwater tanks emit odors into the RV. If this odor is simply because the tank wasn't cleaned properly, then it isn't that big of an issue. However, if it is due to a crack in the tank or a leak in one of the pipes or valves, then it can be quite a hefty problem.

#9 - Heavy Rust

RVs that are kept in cold climates can develop rust on the undercarriage. A light coating isn't an issue, but thick rust can eat through metal. Repairing it is possible, but as you may already expect, it is very expensive.

Rust in the interior is also a major flag since it is a sure sign that water damage has occurred and hasn't been properly addressed. So, the aftermath of mold, leaks, damaged pipes, or appliances covered in water damage could make an appearance. Never purchase an RV with any rust problems no matter whether or not you think you can fix them.

#10 - Body Damage

RVs can be a bit challenging to drive, and they are often damaged naturally as they are used. Small dents and scrapes may not be an issue, but if there are any major signs of body damage such as deep scratches or bent bumpers, you should pass on purchasing.

This could be a sign that the basic structure is damaged internally or isn't built as solidly as you need. In addition, body repairs can be costly.

#11 - Damaged Windshield

Most states have laws against driving a vehicle with any type of windshield damage since it is a danger for travelers. Since RV windshields are large, they can also be costly to replace. Buying an RV with this problem can also increase your insurance rates. So never purchase an RV with windshield damage.

Now you have a good idea of what unit to purchase and perhaps have already made the purchase. If so, I will give you a happy congrats! If you haven't yet, we will cover one more aspect of owning an RV before you can start preparing it for use as your new home. Let's look at the option of a tow vehicle if you choose to purchase a motorhome.

CHOOSING WHETHER OR NOT TO TOW A VEHICLE

If you purchase a motorhome, you will find yourself asking the question: do you really need a tow car? There is no simple answer to this since it depends on your lifestyle and what you plan to do on the road.

Towing a vehicle can be a great way to explore the surrounding area once you set up your basecamp. Unless you have a small RV that can drive around city streets, it can be a waste of gas, time disconnecting, and difficulty driving the RV just to run a quick errand or go see a touristic site.

However, you may not need a tow car if you rarely leave the campground or if you are pulling a trailer camper. It will also depend on your RV type and whether or not it has the ability to tow a car.

If you are going to get a tow vehicle, you need to consider your options for towing systems.

TOWING METHODS

If you want to add a tow vehicle to your plans, there are three ways you can choose for this. Let's look at each of them, as well as their pros and cons. We will also look at how you can choose the right method for your RV.

TOW-BAR TYPE HITCH

Also known as towing 4-down or towing a vehicle with all four wheels on the road is often the preferred method for towing a vehicle behind an RV. This is the easiest way to hook up and unhook a vehicle from a unit.

To tow a car with this method, you'll need a ball hitch or a single-point connection at the RV and a two-point connection system on the tow vehicle. This type of connection allows it to swivel at the RV end while having two stable connections at the vehicle end.

PROS

- This is a convenient system for RV driver since they can even back up a few feet with the vehicle attached if needed.

- After a long drive, it is nice to have a vehicle that can be quickly disconnected from the unit and used to explore the nooks and crannies of a town or city.

- It is an easy option for those who have physical limitations.

CONS

- Vehicles with a front-wheel drive or all-wheel drive can be towed with this system without causing permanent damage.

- Rear-wheel drive vehicles require the installation of a solenoid switch kit, so damage doesn't occur to the vehicle when being towed.

- Some vehicles require a tow-bar adapter to be installed on the front underside of the chassis for safe towing.

TOW DOLLY

A tow dolly is basically a two-wheeled trailer with a "ball hitch" adapter that attaches to your RV. You drive the front wheels of the car onto the trailer; then you use special straps and chains to tie the vehicle to the trailer bed. This makes the front end of the tow car stable on the dolly while the rear wheels are free-wheeling down the road.

PROS

- There is no need for specialized tow-bar adapters or wiring.

- It is easy to hook up the dolly to the RV as long as you can physically lift and drag it to the RV.

CONS

- The cost of tow dolly is higher than the 4-down towing system.

- Backing up with a tow dolly is impossible.

- Loading the vehicle on the tow dolly can take 20 to 30 minutes and requires a good amount of physical labor.

TRAILER

With a trailer, you can easily tow any type of recreational vehicle you want, and it works exactly as it sounds.

PROS

- Trailers are available in nearly any size you need.

- No mechanical or electrical modifications are required.

CONS

- Most campgrounds don't have storage space for extra trailers.

- If there is storage space, you can expect to pay an extra fee.

CHOOSING THE RIGHT METHOD

As you can tell, there are numerous requirements and options available when it comes to choosing a method to tow a vehicle behind your RV. You'll need to do some research to fully inform yourself of which option is more convenient to your preferences. You should also know your RVs towing capacity, so you don't choose the wrong setup and vehicle.

TIPS TO TOWING A VEHICLE

Lastly, I want to share with you some tips and information I've learned after towing a vehicle for a while. This can help you avoid some mistakes and decide if having a tow vehicle is right for you.

- If you are going to get a tow vehicle make sure you choose a car that meets your needs, as we discussed a minute ago.

- If you are going to be off-roading, you want a vehicle with 4-wheel drive.

- If you just want to go outside and enjoy driving to see the scenery, a convertible may be the way to go.

- If you are going to tow with 4-wheels on the ground, make sure the car will work with this method. Also, ensure that towing a vehicle doesn't void the warranty.

- Always have a supplemental braking system installed. This makes it safer and easier in case of an emergency stop or mountain driving. In some states, it may even be required.

- You should consider installing a tire pressure monitoring system. It is important to know the tire pressure and heat spikes in your tires on the tow vehicle while driving your RV.

- Consider installing a rearview camera. This can help you monitor the tow car while driving and see if anything happens.

Once you have all of your vehicles prepared, the first step is to make sure you have appropriate insurance coverage. Then you want to make sure you are prepared and know how to drive the RV as well as know the highway system and what roads to avoid while driving an RV.

RV INSURANCE

Perhaps one of the more confusing aspects of owning an RV is determining appropriate insurance coverage. There are a few choices available, and depending on the RV you choose you may not need RV insurance. Truthfully, RV insurance isn't like home insurance or car insurance. In this section, I'm going to take you through the process of how insurance coverage works, what you need to have, and how you can get it.

WHAT IS RV INSURANCE?

RV insurance is basically protection from loss in relation to your RV and will cover any type of recreational vehicles such as motorhomes, travel trailers, pop-up campers, or anything else in between. The base of RV insurance functions the same as auto insurance, so you'll need to choose a deductible as well as policy limits.

Specific RV insurance policies are a combination of auto insurance and homeowners insurance, meaning it will cover the automotive parts of your RV along with your home belongings inside the vehicle.

DO YOU NEED RV INSURANCE?

The requirements for RV insurance are fairly simple. If you tow your RV, your insurance is optional depending on the state where you live or claim domicile. Although if you are purchasing a trailer through a lender, they may require you to get full insurance coverage in order to secure that RV.

Generally-speaking, it is a good idea to have RV insurance even if it isn't required simply because it is safer for you, particularly when it comes to meeting the state minimum for liability insurance before having the RV on the road.

RV Insurance versus Auto Insurance

While RV insurance is similar to auto insurance, they aren't the same. So, if an auto insurance company wants to issue a traditional insurance policy, there will be gaps in coverage that can be costly and are overall inconvenient.

Auto Insurance

An auto insurance policy is going to treat an RV like a regular car so that it won't cover things such as living spaces, bathrooms, personal possessions, or kitchens. You will basically only be covering the mechanical portion of your RV. While this is the most expensive part of the equation, it would be rather unfortunate if your miscellaneous living items were not accounted for in the case of an accident or a robbery.

RV Insurance

An RV insurance policy is going to cover you for a variety of things you'll have to deal with while on the road, while also covering your personal belongings. It will cover emergency expenses and replacement cost coverage. Needless to say, since auto insurance will only cover part of your living arrangements, you might as well skip a step and get an honest-as-day RV insurance deal.

TYPES OF RV INSURANCE

It is important to know how you plan to use your RV. If you are going to live full-time from your RV, you are going to have different insurance needs over someone who only uses their RV to travel once or twice a year, as you can imagine.

In this scenario, the RV is your home, and you want to make sure your home is covered. A full-time RV insurance policy is going to provide liability coverage as a homeowner's policy does, and it will protect you against losses when using your RV as the primary residence. The policy will also cover medical expenses for those insured in and around the RV along with emergency coverage.

WHAT DOES IT COVER?

Every RV policy is going to work differently, so you want to learn exactly what your specific policy covers. You may need to get additional coverage for custom items in your RV. In general, most policies will cover the following.

Personal Property and Belongings

This covers items while driving and while parked. This typically includes:

- Laptops

- Televisions

- Cell Phones

- Dishware

Policies will differ on the amount of coverage, so check your individual plan for specifics. If you reach your insurance limit, you can consider additional coverage under a homeowner's policy if you still own your home outside of your RV.

Uninsured Motorist Coverage

This works in the same way as a traditional auto insurance policy. If you are in an accident with someone who isn't insured or if you are in a hit and run situation then this part of the policy will protect you.

Personal Attachments Coverage

This coverage protects things attached to your RV such as:

- Satellite Dishes

- TV Antenna

- Awnings

This coverage is important to have, especially if you drive through bad weather or under a bridge that is lower than you thought. Check your policy to make sure you know the limits for how much they will cover for attachments.

Collision Coverage

This part of the policy will cover you for any damage caused to your RV if you are in an accident with another vehicle. This will cover you no matter who is at fault, which is quite handy.

Full Replacement Cost Coverage

Should your RV be destroyed by a covered loss or stolen, you will get your RV replaced with the full 100 percent using this portion of your policy.

Medical Payment Coverage

The portion of this policy will cover the medical expenses for both you and your passengers if the RV is involved in an accident, no matter who is at fault, similar to collision coverage. When looking at your policy options, you should ask about this coverage specifically, as it is an essential type of liability coverage you should have.

Comprehensive Coverage

Will cover your RV for anything outside of a collision and is sometimes referred to as "other than collision" coverage. This will cover your RV from damage from things like:

- Vandalism

- Theft

- Falling objects

- Fire

- Storms

- Floods

- Other natural disasters

With this type of coverage, you need to know your policy limits.

Roadside Assistance

If you travel a specific distance from your home or registered domicile, your roadside assistance will kick in. You may want to consider getting more coverage for this since towing an RV is going to cost a lot more than a regular vehicle.

Roadside assistance covers you if a breakdown occurs because of the following:

- Mechanical or electrical breakdown

- Battery failure

- Flat tire

- Lockout

- Insufficient fuel, oil, water, or other fluids

Pet Injury Coverage

Anyone who has a pet knows that living with them can be a daily adventure. Living with a pet in an RV on the road can be difficult to manage, even when the pet is well-behaved and accustomed to car travel. Ideally, you will have an additional pet insurance policy, but if not, this can be added to your policy for an additional cost, and you'll need to check your policy limits.

HOW MUCH DOES IT COST?

Before we can consider the cost of RV insurance, we first need to look at how the cost structure is determined. There are a few things that can vary the cost:

- Your motorhome or RV class

- How often you use your RV

- Driving history

- Deductibles and limits

- Additional riders

- Your current age

- If you are married or single

- Your gender

- Your insurance credit score

This being said, it is easy to see why policies can vary greatly. Your premiums could easily be between $50 and $22,000 a year depending on those specifications and the company you are trying to get insurance from. It is best to get several quotes and compare options to find a policy that gives you the coverage you need at a price you can afford.

HOW MUCH COVERAGE DO YOU NEED?

As you can tell above, there is a lot that goes into an RV insurance policy. Your need will be based on factors like the following:

- The class of your motorhome

- Where you are going to travel

- If you are traveling full or part-time

- Whether or not you have a custom feature

- What you want to protect with the policy

Although the most simple and direct answer is: you are going to need as much coverage as you can afford. You want to make sure you, your guests, your RV, and your personal property are adequately covered. Once you've evaluated your needs and come up with your own number, you can talk with an agent to get an insurance quote.

UNDERSTANDING THE HIGHWAY SYSTEM

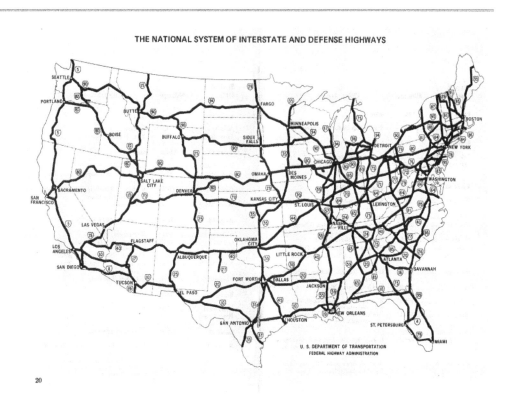

THE NATIONAL SYSTEM OF INTERSTATE AND DEFENSE HIGHWAYS

U. S. DEPARTMENT OF TRANSPORTATION
FEDERAL HIGHWAY ADMINISTRATION

20

While technology can be helpful, if you are retired and traveling the road, it is safe to assume you have a bit of time to spare in your journeys. Try to stop and smell the rose along the way and don't worry much about using a GPS to get to a destination by a specific hour in the day unless you wrote it as part of your itinerary for the week.

Enjoy the scenery and learn to travel by the signs alone, or perhaps with the help of a physical map. It is possible to travel the US Highway System without ever using a map, compass, or another direction device, though. Let's look at what you need to know in order to understand the highway system.

THE BASICS

Knowing the position of the sun is your best way to get a general sense of direction. If you are aware of the sun in the morning and the sunset in the evening, you can follow the general directional guideline. These basic guidelines are the following:

- The sun rises in the East.

- The sun sets in the West.

This can be a problem during cloudy days or places where the sun does not actually set during a particular season, so you should at least bring a map with you regardless of how often you actually use it.

Now let's look at the details of the US highway system.

THE US HIGHWAY SYSTEM

The first thing you want to consider is the numbers. Numbers are key in finding out whether you are on the two-lane US highway or the huge multi-lane traffic of the Interstate Highway System. The US highways take you through history and many of the small towns of America. The interstates are more modern, taking you from city to city at a faster rate. They both use the same system, however.

Route Numbers will tell you how far north or south, east or west you are and give you a rough idea of where you are headed. Mile Markers and Exit Numbers work together to tell you have far you've traveled in a state on a particular road. This makes it possible to travel anywhere without a map or atlas. Again, I highly urge you to bring a map with you just for the purpose of having one available at all times in case of emergencies, unexpected circumstances, or necessary stops.

ROUTE NUMBERS

All highways have route numbers. Occasionally they will have letters, but this simply means you are on a county or state road. The highways and interstates all come with clear rules when it comes to route numbers.

Even versus Odd Numbers

Routes that take you East/West have even numbers such as US 20, which takes you from Boston to Newport, Oregon. North/South routes have odd numbers such as I-95, which takes you along the Atlantic Seaboard.

Numerical Order

This rule varies depending on which highway system you are on, but in general will have the same pattern. The number of the highway will tell you more about the landscape where you are.

For US Highways, east/west routes are numbered from north to south. The lower the number the further up north you are. For example, US Route 10 is closer to Canada than US 20, and US 90 is closer to Mexico than US 80.

North/south routes are the same patterns, with lower numbers in the east and the higher numbers in the west. For example, US Route 1 follows the Atlantic Seaboard, while US 101 takes you down the Pacific Coast. So, if you have a low route number you are either up north on an even route or back east on an odd route.

For Interstates, the same general rule occurs but in the opposite order. I-95 is the highest numbered road in the system and takes you down the East Coast while I-5 takes you through the middle of the Pacific Coast states. I-90 is the farthest north Interstate, while I-10 is down in Texas.

Digits

There are two types of highways; the primary ones are in the ones or tenths range while the Spurs have three digits. For example, primary routes are highways like US 30, US 6, I-10, and I-5.

Spurs have three digits and are typically connected to primary routes. These often provide a route to a nearby city that isn't located along the primary route, or a bypass around downtown or high traffic area.

MILE MARKERS

Now that you know how to tell the longitude and latitude of your travel let's look at how you can tell a specific direction you are traveling.

You can use the sun or read a route sign, but you can also check mile markers, which are typically small green signs with white numbers on them spotted along the roadside. Well-traveled routes will have a marker for every mile, and some Interstates will display them in tenths of miles. On the other hand, some backcountry highways will have them only every 20 miles or so. No matter how far apart they are, you can use them to tell your specific direction.

Mile Markers decrease as the roads travel west or south and increase as you reach the Northeast. For example, if you are driving West on an even-numbered road, the numbers will be getting smaller until you reach a state border. In the new state, the number changes to how many miles along the road is for the particular state.

The same applies when you are driving south. This allows you to tell how much time left you to have in a state by the number of miles left on a road that travels from boundary to boundary in a state.

EXIT NUMBERS

If you don't have Mile Markers, you can use Exit Numbers, which are often aligned with Mile Markers. For example, if you are driving west and you want Exit 109, then you know you have 50 miles to go when you reach Mile Marker 159.

EXCEPTIONS

This highway system isn't perfect and in some situations hasn't been fully implemented. Numerous factors can contribute to the exceptions to the rules.

US 101

This is a primary route despite the three-number designation.

I-99

Although designated I-99, it is further west than I-81 and even further away from I-95 and I-97, which are the easternmost interstate in this country.

I-97

Although not really an exception, I-97 is the only Interstate that runs through a single county. It is also the shortest Primary Interstate Route in the US and the only one that doesn't connect to any other Primary Instate Routes. It travels for 17.62 miles in Anne Arundel County in Maryland.

I-238

This road meets several exceptions. While this should be a bypass or loop, there is no I-38 and if it did exist it should be further south.

DRIVING TIPS

One thing I quickly found out was that driving an RV is nothing like driving a vehicle. Simple things like the right turn and parking required extra practice and nerves of steel. So if you are getting your first RV before you hit the road and start living out of it, it is important you learn how to properly drive the RV in the first place. Here are some of the basics that you may need to reconsider learning in your RV.

TURNING

RVs are long and wide, meaning your turns need to be the same as well. This is especially true for right turns since you're up against a curb. To successfully turn an RV you want to watch your rear-view mirrors and keep as close to the center lane as you can get. Slow down and take your time, don't worry about the traffic behind you.

It is better to take it slow and easy than to have damage to your RV that you'll have to repair or live with or any costly expenses of an unexpected crash.

BRAKING

Braking in a vehicle as heavy and large as an RV will take longer than braking in a normal vehicle, based on common logic. This means you should maintain a greater distance from those in front of you and keep a close eye out for trouble so you can react immediately if needed.

If you are traveling downgrade, make sure you downshift and allow the engine to do as much braking for you as possible. Increased engine resistance in a lower gear will cause your vehicle to slow down while reducing the amount of wear and tear you place on your brakes.

PARKING

When parking an RV, it is important to stop whenever you can't see clearly. If needed, have a spotter to help direct you into the parking spot. Take your time with the parking process and use your mirrors. It is best to avoid tight spots if possible and find an easy parking spot without many other vehicles around you, even if you have to park slightly far away from your destination.

If you need to backup while towing a trailer, remember the trailer is going to turn in the opposite direction of your steering wheel.

LANE POSITION

RVs are wider than you may originally think, and it can be hard to tell how close the passenger side of the vehicle is to the shoulder. Until you are used to it, it can be quite disorienting. In the meanwhile, make sure you watch your mirrors and note how close your back tires come to the lane markers.

Whenever possible, you should stay on the right lane so you can continue driving steadily and focus on the traffic to your left, ensuring it does not get too close to you.

BRIDGES

One of the main things that people forget when driving an RV is bridge clearance. Really establish your RV's height in your mind and on paper, and beware of low bridges. If you have a GPS device make sure you set it to alert you of low bridges and plan your routes around them.

MOUNTAINS AND HIGH GRADES

When driving the mountains, stay slow. Keep your RV in low gear, both uphill and downhill. Stay on the right lane if possible and don't worry about any vehicles that pass you. As you travel downhill, ensure your vehicle doesn't gain too much speed. Instead, keep things in low gear so you can keep the speed of the RV at very low numbers.

STOPPING AT GAS STATIONS

Instead of stopping at a regular gas station, it is best to take your RV to a truck stop. Most standard gas stations don't have the space to accommodate the height and width of an RV. Don't damage your fenders, sides, and roof or take extra time trying to fill up at a normal gas station. It is far easier if you simply skip all the drama and head to a truck stop.

KEEPING AN EYE BEHIND YOU

The most important thing when driving an RV is to remember to take it slow and easy (cannot keep stressing this point enough times) while using your mirrors. Don't feel rushed or like you need to keep up with everyone else; it is better to stay slow. With practice and time, you'll soon be driving your RV naturally and enjoy it every step of the way.

Next, here are a few tips that will help make it easier for you to adjust to RV driving and be successful on the road.

LOTS OF PRACTICE

In many ways, learning to drive an RV is much like when you were learning to drive for the first time. It is going to be clumsy, unwieldy and hard at first, and this is okay. As when you are learning new skills, practice will help you learn faster.

Go to an empty parking lot and just spend some time practicing. Focus on the more difficult techniques such as turns, parallel parking, K-turns, perpendicular parking and other maneuvers you would like to review. You won't be an expert the first time you drive an RV, but with practice and patience, you'll get there in no time.

ADJUST YOUR MIRRORS

When driving an RV one of the biggest challenges is seeing what's behind you. This is why you must have a clear view of what is behind your vehicle at all times. Therefore, it is important that you adjust your mirrors before heading out on the road and don't be afraid to pull over any time you need to re-adjust them.

However, this process is a little more involved than you may think. So let's take a side trip here for a moment to learn how you can adjust your mirrors.

A motorhome typically has a pair of two-piece mirrors on two adjustable arms at the front of the rig. Before you start adjusting your mirrors you want to remember that these mirrors extend outside of an already-wide vehicle.

So look down the edge of your RV and always adjust the mirrors so that the edge of the mirrors align with the side of your rig and no further. Since most RVs are at eight feet, six inches wide, which is the legal limit in most states. If your mirrors extend beyond those measurements, they will be the first thing hit when parking or driving your RV.

Oftentimes the lower smaller mirrors are fixed and need to be set manually outside the RV. The larger upper mirrors are often adjustable from inside the RV. However, you may occasionally find an RV where these positions are reversed. If you have never adjusted your RV mirrors before, you'll need to take the following steps:

1. Sit in the driver's seat while someone else adjusts the mirror frame to where it is described below.

2. Loosen the lock-down bolts on the frame of the mirror and pre-set the frame where you want it. Then pre-set the adjustable and fixed mirrors to the middle of their range.

3. Once you are close, lock the mirror frame bolts down. These often use an Allen wrench, and you should have this in your toolbox.

4. The larger top mirrors are not magnifiers and provide you with a larger field of view of the road behind you. These mirrors should be set to allow the driver to see the edge of the RV as well as down the road from a point about halfway down the body of the RV.

5. Lastly, the lower and smaller mirrors are magnifiers and provide a smaller field of view. The edge should be set

further in so the driver can see the bottom of the RV about eight to ten feet behind them.

Setting the mirrors in this manner will provide the driver with a decent view of nearly all vehicles that might be driving behind and beside the RV. Let's consider a few helpful tips.

MARK THE LOCATION OF THE REAR WHEEL

A little trick to help with the mirrors involves three steps:

1. While you are in the driver's seat, have your navigator stand beside the rear tire on one side of the RV.

2. Place a small mark on the mirror where their knees are.

3. Place a small colored dot on the mark and repeat for the other side.

This will help when parking your RV since it will give you a good indication of where the rear tires are. This will be very helpful if your wheel wells are hard to see in the mirror.

Mark for Lane Changing

Another helpful tip will help when changing lanes. Often, even if you have a rearview camera, it can be challenging to change lanes after passing a vehicle, especially if you are towing a vehicle. If so, follow these steps:

1. If you have a tow vehicle, have your navigator stand parallel to the rear of the tow vehicle.

2. Place a mark on the larger mirror at the knees and then place a colored dot on that spot.

3. Repeat with the other mirror.

You can then use the dot to tell you when you are a decent distance beyond and safe to return to the lane.

Now that you have your mirrors adjusted let's get back to some more driving tips for your RV.

KEEP AN EYE ON THE WEATHER

You can't expect perfect weather all the time when you are living in a physical house, much less when you are living in an RV. In order to avoid driving in harsh conditions like heavy rain, strong winds, thunderstorms, and lightning, or snow, you should have a decent weather app you can rely on.

This way you can plan your escape routes beforehand, if you will. Be smart about when to stop your travels for the day. If you get surprised in any of these weather conditions, you may want to consider finding a safe place to pull over for a while and move on when your surroundings area bit calmer.

NEVER DRIVE IF YOU ARE TIRED

This is pretty much common sense, but it is important to mention. If you live in an RV, a large part of your time is going to be spent traveling from Point A to B. Sometimes this distance can be hundreds of miles and sometimes even traveling across states. You may have a set schedule to stick to, but don't ignore feelings of fatigue.

Driving with any level of fatigue in an RV can be dangerous and even fatal. You need to have your full attention on driving, especially if you are a first-time RV driver. So if you are feeling tired, don't push through it; find a place to park and spend the night or let your passenger drive while you take a break.

KNOW YOUR LIMITS

Your travels are likely to take you on a number of different roads including bridges, tunnels, and overpasses. Before you head on the road, make sure you have measurements for your RV. The most important measurements are width and height.

The typical height is 11 to 13 feet, and you should keep this number in mind for tunnels and overpasses. If you can, plan your trip to avoid places that won't accommodate your RV, and if you find yourself coming upon one, then use a GPS to find an alternate route.

BE COURTEOUS

When driving an RV, you'll always be sharing the road with up to hundreds of drivers at a time, depending on how major the road you are traveling on at the time is. In other words, you ought to be courteous. Keep in mind that you are in a larger and less common vehicle so other motorists may be nervous driving around you.

Therefore, it helps to be polite. If you need to merge, turn on your signal and gradually merge. This allows others plenty of time to make room for you and reduce the risk of accidents. Knowing your route can also help you to signal as early as possible.

STAY TO THE RIGHT

Unless you are driving in another country, motorists stay in the right lane. For an RV driver, this is even truer. An RV is going to be a slow-moving, large vehicle and other cars are likely going to be passing you. Stay out of other people's way and don't slow down the rest of the traffic by staying in the far right lane.

This will also keep you closer to the shoulder should any mechanical issues come up while you're driving. The exception would be if you are on a highway with exit ramps. In these instances, you can move left one lane until all cars have passed on the exit ramp and then move back to the right lane.

BRAKE AT THE RIGHT TIME

This is another one that likely seems like a common sense situation, but it is important to mention. The average RV is heavy, standing at over 5,000 pounds. You need to account for the weight of your supplies as well.

Braking in an RV is far different from that of a car or truck; there is no such thing as braking suddenly with this kind of vehicle. In addition to being alert and courteous at all times, you need to plan out your braking in advance. It will take a while for your vehicle to come to a complete stop, so you should make sure the path in front of you is always clear.

MAINTAIN A SAFE DISTANCE

It is always recommended you don't get too close to other vehicles when driving an RV. It is best to stay separated by at least 400 feet, but 500 is even better. If you can't visualize this, count at least four seconds and then you know you are far enough away from other vehicles (six seconds would be even better). This is the minimum amount of distance you'll need to brake safely without hitting others. If someone pulls in on you, then simply hold back more.

REMEMBER TAIL SWING

Before you get into an RV for the first time, you want to understand tail swing, which is defined as "the distance that the body of the coach behind the pivot point moves in the opposite direction of the front when you turn." If you don't have a motorhome, remember that the longer part of the vehicle won't turn at the exact same time as the front. You need to plan for and accommodate this distance gap. You can achieve this by calculating your exact tail swing.

You can do this by finding an empty street or parking lot. Pull your RV up flush with the white line. Use this line as a reference point for turning. Have your navigator watch as you turn to calculate the tail swing.

The average tail swing is between 18 and 30 inches, but they can easily be more or less depending on the size of your RV and how tight you turn. Once you know your number, keep it in mind and get comfortable with it since you'll be using it often. The more practice you have driving, the more comfortable you'll be with making tight and loose turns.

Owning an RV is wonderful, but driving one can be a little stressful under most circumstances, especially if it is your first time. Remember that if you just practice and take the tips above in mind, you'll soon become a natural and remain safe during your travels.

CAMPSITE PARKING AND AVOIDANCE

Driving an RV is challenging, but it is even more difficult to park it at the end of the day. You need to make sure you know how to safely and accurately back into a campsite even if it is difficult to determine exactly where the rear end and rear wheels are on a large RV. I'm going to tell you a simple three-step procedure I've learned that makes it easier to back your RV into place on the first try. It might ring a bell, as it is very similar to the three-point steps we mentioned earlier to keep a safe distance from cars and to set your mirrors.

Go to an office supply store and buy some stick-on colored dots. Then head back to your RV and do three things:

1. On the driver's side of your RV measure from the center of the left-rear drive tire to a point about eight feet forward on the RV body. This is an important alignment point for the RV to start the turn into a parking site.

2. At this point, place one of the stick dots near eye level so the navigator who is guiding you into the campsite or parking spot will be able to see it easily. This is a reference point for the first step of the three-step process for backing into a campsite or parking spot.

3. Repeat this same process on the passenger side for those times when you'll need to back into a spot on the opposite side of the street.

Now you are prepared and ready to back your RV into a campsite or parking spot using the following three steps. Here we like to do things in a series of three, as it makes matters far easier to remember. Bear with me for a moment as you:

#1 - DEFINE A LINE

Communication between you and your navigator is crucial throughout this process. So you should either develop a set of hand signals or use walkie-talkies to clearly communicate directions. The navigator will have to be outside the RV and directing the driver throughout the whole process. The navigator should move around as needed so the driver can see them at all times.

To start, the navigator needs to define a line into the campsite that is one foot inside the edge of the campsite or parking spot. This is where the RV tires are going to end up after parking. The navigator should stand on this line at the front edge of the campsite and hold their arms out straight in front to indicate the street edge of the campsite.

Once the navigator is in place, the driver should pull forward slowly, keeping the body of the RV almost touching the hands of the navigator until they drop their arms, indicated that the marker dot is right where their hands are.

#2 - PULL FORWARD

This is where you will get your RV aligned so you can turn into the campsite. Continuing from your position in the first step, the driver needs to turn the steering wheel fully to the right, then pull forward until they have crossed the street as far as possible. Once here, stop the RV. In streets of typical width, your right rear tire should be on or near the imaginary line at the front corner of the campsite.

#3 - BACK INTO THE SITE

Now you can be a position to back into the campsite or parking spot without overshooting the entrance. Turn the steering wheel fully to the left and start to back up the RV. The driver can adjust the steering as needed to remain on a straight line into the campsite until the front tires are on the imaginary line. Now that the RV is in the campsite, the driver can straighten the wheel and back straight into the campsite or parking spot.

This three-step process works great for those who are new to driving an RV; you might develop a system that works better for you once you gain more experience and practice with driving an RV. This three-step process will save you a lot of time getting into narrow parking areas as a whole. If you have a rear camera use it along with your mirrors as a tool while you are backing up, so you don't hit anything or misalign your RV.

Once you are aligned, your navigator can help you move forward or backward until your slides and awnings don't hit anything while opening. You'll also want to make sure your service lines and cables are accessible and within easy distance for a hookup.

HELPFUL TIPS FOR BACKING UP A TRAILER

When towing a trailer, it can be even more difficult to get into a campsite or parking space, as well as parallel parking.

Again, it will be helpful to have a helper since they can stand behind the trailer and use hand signals to help keep the trailer aligned as it fits into the spot. For an extra safety measure, it is always recommended to use Walkie Talkies or cell phone calls in order to get very clear instructions from the person behind the RV toward the driver.

PIVOT POINT

A lot of it depends on the distance from the pivot point of the trailer or the hitch to the wheels of the trailer. This pivot point will determine how easy it is to back up the trailer. If the distance of the pivot point is short, then the trailer is going to react very fast and extreme when you turn your steering wheel. So it is important that you back up slowly and turn the wheel slightly to adjust alignment properly.

If you have a longer trailer or a fifth wheel, then it will be easier to back up and park.

STEERING IN THE OPPOSITE DIRECTION

The other thing you need to master is turning the steering wheel in the opposite direction of where you want the trailer to go. After you get used to this, the entire process of backing up a trailer will be a lot easier.

The key to all of this is, do you have a guess? That's right. The key is to take it slow. When you take your time, it will go smoothly, and you'll be able to get it right on the first try.

When you are driving a car, you often don't have to give much thought to the roads you take. However, there are four types of roads you should try to avoid when you are driving an RV.

City Streets. Larger cities are great for walking around and seeing the sights, but the traffic congestion makes for difficult driving in an RV. Also the narrow lanes, an abundance of turns and a sheer number of vehicles and pedestrians will make it challenging for even experienced RV drivers. If you plan on visiting a large city, you should consider leaving your RV parked somewhere safe and take another form of transportation during your stay in the actual city or town.

Interstates. The interstate is a great way to get to your destination sooner and faster, but it can also be pretty boring if you have time to spare and want to enjoy your surroundings. Remember, you are retired, and it is all about the journey. So take the back roads and enjoy the local flavor around you.

Coastal Roads, Mountain Trails, and Cliff Drives. These are iconic in a lot of ways and great for a day drive, but they often aren't designed for larger vehicles like RVs. Things like hairpin turns can be difficult to make in an RV, especially if you are towing a vehicle. There are even some scenic routes that prohibit large vehicles. If they are legal to drive, then be prepared for a scary experience. Or, to avoid all of that struggle, avoid all of these and use a rental car instead, or go hiking on foot, horseback, or bicycle while your RV is parked somewhere else in a safer location.

Poorly Maintained Roads. While this may not seem like an issue during actual driving, it can be an issue for other parts of your vehicle. Consider the number of things that can rattle loose on a bumpy road like pebbles or stones and twigs or branches. There are a number of things that can be damaged.

PREPARING THE LOGISTICS OF FULL-TIME RV LIVING

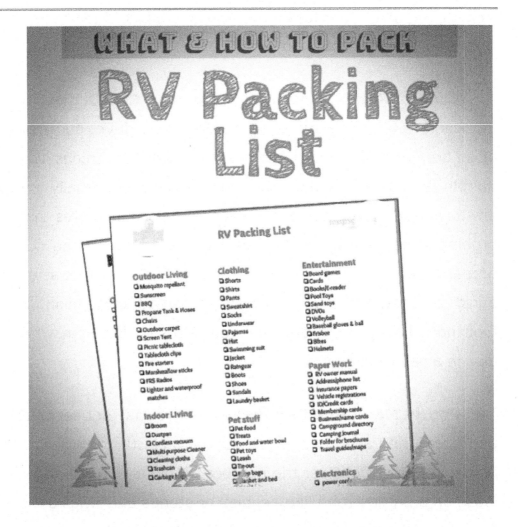

So now you have your RV, you've downsized your possessions, and you've learned how to drive the vehicle; what's next? There are a lot of logistics that go into full-time RV living, as you may have already noticed in previous chapters.

You need to know what and how to pack, you need to set up your utilities, and learn how you are going to live on the road with all the necessities that you would have in a normal home. So let's get into the logistics of living full-time in an RV. We'll start with what and how you need to pack your RV.

WHAT TO PACK IN AN RV

When you are preparing to live in an RV, one of the biggest challenges you will face after downsizing your possessions is to determine what you need to bring with you in your RV and how to pack it all. The downsizing process was likely more difficult than you thought and even then you'll probably find you've made some mistakes. You may want to take a few trips in your RV first to see just what you need. If you require a bit of help, look at the following tips.

YOU DON'T NEED THAT MANY SUPPLIES AND TOOLS

You should start by packing the basic items needed to operate the RV. This includes the following:

☐ Wheel Chocks

☐ Leveling Blocks

☐ Sewer Hose

☐ Fresh Water Hose

☐ Propane

☐ Tire Inflator

Some extra items you may choose to pack depending on your individual needs include the following:

☐ Tow Bar

☐ Extra Storage Rack

☐ Solar Panels

It is best to avoid packing larger items that can be easily bought if you need them, especially if you have limited space. It can be easy to overbuy when it comes to accessories for your RV. It is best to simply pack the bare minimum and then purchase more as you go and find you need other things as you go along. It is easier to deal with this than having too much packed into your RV at once.

Perhaps one of the biggest mistakes that new RVers make it packing too many tools. Not only will you not use most of these items, but their weight will just add extra pounds to your RV. Later in this book, we are going to look at maintenance and repairs.

CONSIDER WHERE YOU PLAN TO STAY

While you'll be traveling a lot, there will be times where you're going to park and stay in one particular location for a while. Whether you are choosing to stay at RV parks or boondock, knowing exactly where you are going to stop will determine a lot of what you want to pack.

For example, if you plan to boondock or dry camp whenever you stop in a place for a while, you are going to need additional camping supplies that people who are staying in RV parks wouldn't necessarily need to pack.

THE COMFORTS OF HOME

Everyone is going to have a hobby or that one item/thing that they need to have. It is best to make room for these items and take them with you. Having your hobby or small collection is going to make it easier for you to be relaxed and happily live life on the road. Even if space is limited, it is important to treat yourself to the comforts of home.

My wife still has her wire-weaving supplies in a tiny kit she opens when we go on long drives, so she is able to keep making pieces of jewelry with stones we find along the coast or on lakes, and if any of her supplies run out, we can always buy more at a local store. I personally am a fan of Sudoku puzzles, but since we don't always find Sudoku puzzle books in the towns we go to, I have an app just for that saved up on my phone when I have a chance to be on a small break.

EVERYDAY ITEMS

Most RVs will come with the basics such as furniture, TV sets and appliances, but there are many items you'll want to pack to make your surroundings more livable, functional, and comfortable. Depending on your individual needs and tastes you may need to add more things than others, but the final deciding factor on what you pack will depend on the size and design of your RV.

For example, if your unit comes with carpeting, then you'll need to pack a vacuum while an RV with no carpeting won't need a vacuum.

HOUSEHOLD ITEMS

You are going to need basic household items such as dishes, cooking utensils, pots, and pans. How much and what you pack will depend on your cooking style and how often you cook versus eating out at some locations. You will also need items to clean the unit such as paper goods, plastic ware, and linens. However, there are also ways to limit the amount of these items you have on hand to reduce what you keep on board.

An example would be to have a place serving for four, along with a supply of paper and plastic kitchenware. This way you will always have enough dishware to serve everyone without taking up the space of full dishware. It is best to choose items like Corning ware that is lightweight, stackable, and unbreakable.

SMALL APPLIANCES

Some people like to use their stoves and ovens in the RV and others don't. It depends on your comfort level using propane and may require you to carry extra cleaning products as well. If this is the case, you may choose to equip yourself with a range of small appliances. Small appliances are easier to manage, store, and clean up. We'll discuss this in greater detail when we talk about cooking in your RV in a later chapter.

SEWER CLEANING EQUIPMENT AND CHEMICALS

We are going to look at how to dump and clean the sewer tank later, but right now I want to discuss the items you'll need to pack for this. Most RVs come with a special hose that connects to the RV sewer tank. However, you'll also need to pack water and garden hoses, protective gloves, donuts, tank cleaning chemicals, and pressure cleaning wands in order to properly clean your sewer system.

ELECTRIC WIRES AND ADAPTERS

When living in your RV, it is extremely important that you are able to hook up to electricity. Most RV parks have a variety of choices for this, so you'll need to make sure you keep adapters and wires on hand so you can properly connect no matter what. Most small RVs need 30 amp connectors while larger RVs have 50 amp connections. If you have an adapter for both wires, you'll never be without an electrical connection.

A Campground Guide

It is always a good idea to have a campground guide book with you at all time. It provides you with the contact information you need for campgrounds as well as other helpful information to ensure you find the right site. Most RV guides will also show you where to get repairs nearly anywhere in the United States.

Outdoor Furniture

Nearly all campgrounds provide picnic tables, but we must take into account the few that don't. Therefore, it may be a good idea to pack a few lightweight outdoor chairs and at least a small folding table to set up a decent campsite wherever you find yourself.

Anything beyond this is likely to take up too much space. If you are the sort that would just prefer to set up cloth on the ground or the grass or sit at a tree stump, then none of this is necessary, and you are good to go.

The rest of what you pack is pretty much up to you. If you can find a place in your RV and you are going to use it on a daily basis, bring it along. Just remember to stay within weight limits for your RV since you'll be surprised how fast weight can add up.

You also must avoid clutter. Make sure everything has a spot and that it won't get broken when you travel. The more clutter you have, the smaller space may seem. So hopefully these tips will help you get a better idea for what you should pack. Now it is important to talk about how to pack your RV when you are ready to head down the road.

How to Pack an RV

Learning how to pack your RV is just as important as what you pack in your RV. This is for both comfort and safety reasons. Since you are using your RV as your home, it is easy to forget that it is also a vehicle that needs to be well-balanced in order to travel safely on roads and highways. There are two main dangers you are avoiding when packing properly:

1. Uneven packed RV don't travel well on slippery roads, and they don't do well on roads under construction.

2. Also, an RV that isn't packed well makes it more difficult to find things and leaves you more likely to forget items you need.

This is why you want to pack your RV carefully. Comfort and safety are very important when living on the road. So let's look at what you need to do in order to get packing right.

Why It's Important

An RV that isn't balanced will be both dangerous and awkward to drive. An improperly packed RV can also make life miserable. Nothing is worse than finding yourself with an overturned RV, and you don't want the discomfort of using the bathroom only to realize you don't have any toilet paper. You won't have to worry about either of these issues with the following organization and planning tips.

How to Balance Your RV

The key to balancing your RV is to keep it bottom heavy and make sure the items you pack are evenly distributed over the axles. The important five tips to remember for this are the following:

1. Check the manual to determine how much weight each axle can carry.

2. Weight your empty RV on a certified scale at a truck stop.

3. Pack your RV with the heavier items down low and spread out evenly along the length of the RV.

4. Re-weigh the RV.

5. Make any needed adjustments.

Often the heaviest items in an RV are going to be the appliances, slide rooms, engine, generator, and water tanks. When you weigh the RV, you'll see which axles are carrying the most weight. Once you have this information, you can pack light where the RV is the heaviest and pack heavy where the weight in the RV is the lightest. You should also pack light items up higher and heavy items down lower. When you do this, your RV will be less likely to turn over since you'll be able to have better control of your RV.

TIPS FOR BETTER PACKING

When you are living in an RV, you are already living a minimalist lifestyle and likely don't have many possessions. You'll also likely have mostly small items that can double for different roles. You may have that one pot that cooks several items and also serves to transport water, etc. Overdoing the items in your RV will have it feeling claustrophobic and uncomfortable, causing you to spend the majority of your time looking for Knickknacks that are only specifically used for a single thing.

There are numerous ways in which people pack for travel. Eventually, you find a system that works for you and the items you have. Knowing where you plan to travel and how long you'll stay in an area can also help you plan for what you will purchase during your visit and what you'll need to pack with you to get you to your next point for stocking.

STORE IN YOUR TOW VEHICLE

You can also use a tow vehicle for extra storage and a place to keep non-perishable items if you need extra room in your RV. No matter where you pack things, keep track of where you put them. This way you won't have to spend valuable time looking for these tools in the first place.

Having lists and written instruction//indications of where every item is at (or should be at) is extremely helpful as well. That way, if something goes missing, it is either because it was misplaced, or it was forgotten outside your vehicle

UTILITY SOURCES

Perhaps one of the biggest logistics questions many RV travelers have when they first hit the road is how they access basic utilities. This is an important subject since there are going to be times when your RV isn't hooked up to these basic utilities, and yet you are still going to need to operate things like the AC, the kitchen and the bathroom.

The main reason for this is because the RV is a self-contained vehicle with most utility and plumbing systems that can function on their own for a short period of time. This is something we've already talked about earlier in this book under how an RV works.

However, some RVs will have more systems with others. The basic systems all RVs have is holding tanks, propane tanks, batteries, and basic plumbing systems; it is these that provide access to water, some level of power, and the basic bathroom facilities when not hooked up at an RV park. Other RV units come with or can be upgraded to include generators, solar panels, and inverters that provide a greater level of electricity when not connected. The more access you have to basic utilities, the more comfortable life in your RV is going to be.

A SMALL APARTMENT ON WHEELS

Most RVs are designed to be similar to a small apartment on wheels. In addition to being self-contained, a lot of RVs come with their own heating and air conditioning systems. Size and design will determine the number of utilities an RV has, and since an RV is stationary, this also means that they have several methods to use for accessing utilities. This includes connecting at campgrounds and RV parks with a hose and wires or relying on their own internal sources.

THE PLUMBING SYSTEM

The plumbing system in an RV is remarkably similar to that of a house. However, they are made from thinner materials and function a little bit differently, meaning they require a little more care. Gray and black water tanks hold waste in an enclosed area and are built into RVs. The fresh water tank is filled up in a campground and used as needed until it is emptied as gray water.

With a hose attached to the built-in black tank, you are able to release the contents into a sewer outlet by pulling a handle. If the RV isn't hooked up, then the waste can be stored in the tanks until you find a place to dump them. We'll discuss more about this later.

UTILITY HOOKUPS AT A CAMPGROUND OR PARK

Most campgrounds and parks provide you with a utility connection for your RV. Dry camping is the term for those who stay where there are no hookups available; this is typical at truck stops and BLM camping areas. Even if areas don't provide a sewer connection, they do usually offer a place to dump waste.

UTILITY SOURCES ON BOARD

If you aren't at a place with hookups or perhaps the place where you are staying only has limited hookups, then you need to rely on the self-contained systems of the RV. Let's look at your options.

Propane

If you plan to dry camp a lot, you will need to refill your propane tanks quite often. Most campgrounds, truck stops, and gas companies can fill them at a price of about $3 per gallon. A gallon of propane will typically last you about an hour.

Batteries

An RV has two types of batteries: engine and coach. An RV uses the batteries to run internal lighting and to energize the engine. You will need to maintain these batteries and replace them on occasion, but without a battery, your RV can't function.

Solar Panels

Some RVs come with solar panels, or you can upgrade them with a simple kit. Installing these panels on the roof of your RV will trickle a small amount of electricity into the vehicle. This can help power inverters that are used to run TVs and some small appliances. This can also save you money on having to use as much propane.

Generators

A generator can be run on propane gas, or diesel and give you electricity when you aren't hooked up at a park or campground.

Inverters

Inverters receive power from batteries, generators, running engines, and solar panels. They provide enough electricity to run small appliances, fans, heating pads, and TVs. This can help you save money on fuels that run generators.

INTERNET CONNECTIONS

One of the biggest struggles you'll face in an RV is staying connected. It isn't as complicated as it may seem, though. I'm going to address your main options and provide you with some clarity to help you see how you want to proceed.

When it comes to internet connections in your RV you want to find the right option where you don't overpay, don't get burdened with unnecessary services, and don't get poor results. Let's look at the major options for mobile internet in the RV living world and what they offer you. This won't be a comprehensive guide, as we are just discussing your main options. You may find a better deal if you are going to stay in a regional area most of the time and have a better local option.

While traveling in your RV, you have three main ways to access the internet:

1. Public/Private Internet Networks

2. Satellite Connections

3. Wireless Service Provided through Cell Phone Networks

PUBLIC/PRIVATE INTERNET NETWORKS

These internet access points are available throughout the United States. However, the connections and associated speeds are hit or miss. You can improve your overall experience with some additional equipment installed in your RV. There are three primary places where you can get free internet connections while on the road.

Public Libraries

This option is 100 percent free, and the computers come with it. However, you won't be able to use your phone. At a public library, you won't be required to purchase anything in order to use the internet, plus they are available in nearly every town, so it is a consistent option. If you choose to rely on this alternative, then you can also avoid packing a computer in your RV since you can use the ones at the library.

There will be some libraries in larger towns that require you to ask for a guest password in order to use the internet, and there may be a time limit, however.

Local Cafes

This option may be a little harder to find and may not always have internet options, but if you do find one, you get the benefit of enjoying local culture while also enjoying a specialty coffee or dessert. You may want to call or ask around first before heading to a place only to find they don't have internet available.

This can also be a more comfortable option if you need to spend more time on the internet. If you have a data plan that does not require internet, you can also search for locations on your cell phone or through Google Maps.

Coffee and Fast Food Chains

This is the most consistent and available option. However, you may have to deal with a very busy and crowded atmosphere. A lot of chain businesses such as McDonalds and Starbucks offer free internet at all of their locations and can typically be found along major highways. This can be a great place to stop in for a quick snack, coffee, water, and an internet connection.

It may not be the best place to settle in and do all of your banking and private needs since they are chain businesses, but you will know what to expect since they will all be pretty much the same wherever you go.

Satellite Connections

Having a satellite dish for your RV can allow you to stream uploads and downloads through the same connection as your TV. However, this option tends to require more equipment and higher expenses than other options.

WIRELESS SERVICE PROVIDERS

You can use a stand-alone device with mobile internet, or you can use your smartphone with a wireless connection device to send and receive data. However, your service in this instance will rely heavily on your coverage and the quality of the network you are using. It can also be a cost-effective and easy way to get the internet while you're living on the road.

Take a look at the following chart for a comparison of your top options, although there may be some local options that work better for you if you plan to stay in one area for a longer period of time.

Carrier	Prepaid	Monthly Use/Lose	Contract Option	3G Speeds	4G Speeds	Shared Data
True Connect	X			X		
Verizon		X	X	X	X	X
AT&T		X	X	X	X	X
Sprint		X	X	X	X	X
T-Mobile		X	X	X	X	

Vi rgin		X		X	X	
M illenico m		X		X	X	

This section just touches on the basics. You may find a better option, or you may find a combination of options that work best for you when staying connected on the road. Simply choose what is best for you at a price you can afford.

Also, take in mind you may not want to stay connected to the internet while you are driving. You could always just be disconnected during your drive until you reach a more urban setting in order to give yourself a break from social media, emails, or alarmingly gory online news. Instead of scrolling through a social platform, just stare out the window or read that book you always say you want to check out but rarely had the time to do so.

See, you will find that even if you are not connected to the internet, the world will continue to smoothly spin on its own axis and no catastrophes will occur.

HEALTH CARE & GETTING YOUR MAIL

A full-time RVer already has a lot of their plate. You need to keep up with regular maintenance on your RV, and you need to plan out your next stop and place to stay. Plus there are the everyday aspects of living such as cooking, cleaning, and shopping. Not to mention setting aside time to actually enjoy your retirement and have some fun. Perhaps the fact that you are enjoying life is one of the main reasons why you need to prioritize your medical insurance.

Choosing and getting health insurance is a difficult process in normal circumstances, but finding it for those who live from an RV full-time can be even more challenging. You need to find the right insurance coverage that will cover you everywhere you travel in your RV. Healthcare isn't the simplest topic, and this chapter is going to help you tackle this.

HEALTH INSURANCE FOR FULL-TIME TRAVEL

The first thing we need to do is start with the basics. What is it you want to get from a healthcare plane when you live from an RV full-time? Perhaps the first and most important thing is you want coverage that is nationwide or maybe even internationally-acknowledged.

While there are special travel insurance plans for specific trips, this isn't really helpful for someone living in their RV full-time. You are living on the road all the time, and you want a health care plan that will meet your needs without an end date. There are a few options available for you.

YOUR BEST OPTIONS

Since most RVers are either freelance, self-employed, or retired, they will need to buy their health insurance through the marketplace or open enrollment through the Affordable Care Act. You can search for the Affordable Care Act marketplace and enroll. However, there are a few things you need to know before you buy health insurance and head out on the road.

First, your options for healthcare will depend on where you establish your state of residency. We are going to discuss this logistics issue later.

Second, you need to be aware that not all plans will cover you everywhere you go. In fact, if you find a plan that does cover you everywhere, then you've found the exception rather than the rule. Thankfully, one of the most popular states for residency is also one of the best for healthcare plans: Florida.

RV HEALTH INSURANCE

Florida offers some serious benefits for those who establish residency in the state while living in their RV full-time. Florida doesn't have an income tax, has affordable vehicle registration fees, and is popular among RVers, so it has several pre-established mail forwarding services in order for anyone to easily establish a permanent address. It is also the state that offers the cheapest and most comprehensive health insurance for RVers, so you are covered no matter where you go.

Another challenging option for full-time RV living is to deal with your incoming mail. You could have someone gather it for you, but then they have the expense of forwarding it over. There are many mail forwarding services, but they can be costly. So what can you do? Let's look at all your options, and this will help you see what is the best choice available.

WHERE TO HAVE YOUR MAIL DELIVERED?

1. You can have a family member or friend receive and forward your mail.

Pros: This option is cheap as it costs you nothing more than postage.

Cons: Your friends and family can get tired of doing this, and if they move, then you lose your permanent address. Therefore, this option is best for short-term use only.

2. You can rent a box at a local UPS store.

Pros: This option is easy to set up, provides personal service and ensures your packages are handled properly.

Cons: However, this option can be expensive and in some cases may not be viewed as a legal address.

3. You can use a professional mail forward service.

Pros: This ensures professional service that is personal and provides a range of available options. You can often find a service that is available at a reasonable price, and it often provides you with a legal and permanent address.

Cons: On the other hand, this often requires club membership.

Once your mail is collected, you also need to consider how it will be delivered to you and where you plan to pick it up once it arrives. There is no single way to answer this, as each individual has different needs.

You need to consider how fast and how often you need your mail. You also want to keep in mind your budget and how much you are willing to spend. Lastly, you want to take in mind how long you plan to stay in one spot in order to receive mail for a specific period of time. Let's look at the options for where you can collect your mail.

1. You can have it sent to the campground or park where you are staying.

    Pros: This is a convenient option, and you can receive items of all sizes from all mail services.

    Cons: Many campgrounds won't allow this, and even if they do it doesn't guarantee your privacy and security.

2. You can have your mail delivered by general delivery.

    Pros: This is a safe option since your mail is in the post office and can be held up to 30 days if you don't get there that often. It is also available pretty much anywhere.

Cons: Not all post offices will accept general delivery and usually won't take UPS and FedEx deliveries.

3. Lastly, you can have mail sent to a UPS store.

Pros: This is another safe and secure option that allows you to receive packages from all carriers.

Cons: It can be expensive with locations difficult to come by so you will need to coordinate them in advance. Plus, you may have to change if a franchise ever goes out of business.

In the end, choosing a mail forwarding service is an individual option. You will need to consider your own personal needs and wants. Other things to consider include price, convenience and customer service. In theory, you can forward all of your paper mail to the electronic realm, like email. If you decide to order a package online, that's when this becomes a more desirable course of action.

FINDING ENTERTAINMENT

When it comes to entertainment onboard your RV you need to learn about RV antennas, TV signal boosters, and satellite receivers. Most RVs these days come with a wide range of electronic entertainment. Most entry-level RVs have a TV, an AM/FM receiver, and DVD players. Some higher end RVs may come with flat screen TVs, surround sound systems, and auto-tracking satellite receivers.

Most of the audio and visual systems in RVs are the same as the ones you may already have at home. This means you don't need to know much about how to operate them; other than learning which remote control operates what; there isn't much else you need to learn.

However, there are some things you want to keep in mind to ensure you always have a good signal for your onboard entertainment if that is what you desire. If you are the sort, who prefers to stay clear from TVs or entertainment electronics, feel free to skip this section and move along onto the next chapter.

RV ANTENNA

Most RVs have a roof mounted TV antenna. When in the stowed position, it is flat and barely noticeable. However, it also won't give you any signal when stowed either. In order for the antenna to work you need to crank the handle mounted on the ceiling and raise it into operating position.

This is a directional antenna, and it needs to be pointed toward the television station you want to watch in order to get reception. Don't commit the main mistake a lot of RVers make and forget to lower your antenna when you leave. The antenna is constructed from lightweight aluminum tubing and plastic pieces, so leaving it extended means it will be easily broken at the first hint of contact.

To stow your antenna before leaving, simply point it in the correct position as indicated by an arrow near the hand crank. If the antenna isn't centered properly then it won't retract all the way, and it can snap off while lowering it. Consider using a checklist or hanging some kind of reminder, so you don't forget to stow your antenna before getting back on the road.

RV Signal Booster

This is another device that helps improve the TV signal in your RV. This signal booster is typically located near your TV. The coax cable goes from your TV to the signal booster, which gets a signal from the antenna. This booster typically operates on 12-volt DC and has a red indicator light to signify that you have turned on the unit. Without the signal booster on, you typically won't have usable reception.

Another concerning factor about the signal booster is the fact that it uses electricity. It is easy to forget about the signal booster and leave it turned on, which will drain the RV battery. If you are staying at an RV campground or park that provides cable TV, you can hook up the coax cable from the connection outside, and you won't need anything else. Just turn on your TV, and you're good to go.

RV Satellite Receiver

You may want a satellite receiver if you are traveling in an RV full-time. These units are nice since they come with an auto-tracking, in-motion RV satellite. However, these units can be a bit costly. With this option, it will only take you a few minutes each night to dial in the satellite and get reception.

Another option you have is to purchase an antenna tripod. You can set this up on the ground and stabilize it with a gallon milk jug full of water. This will prevent it from tipping over in the wind.

This is all you really need to know about establishing your entertainment center while living out of your RV. There are still a few other logistics we need to consider, so let's dig right into it.

BANKING, TAXES & RESIDENCY

When you live on the road, full-time you are also going to need to think about changing your banking and tax habits. So, how can you ensure that you are meeting all of your financial needs on time? Modern banking, including internet banking, makes it far easier to manage your finances while on the road. The first step you need to take is determining what bank you want to use.

ATM MACHINES AND GETTING CASH

If you plan to use ATMs often to get access to cash, you should consider choosing a bank that is part of a national chain such as Chase or Bank of America. This will save you some money in out-of-town ATM fees. If you plan to use cards mostly, you won't need much cash. This can also be a safer approach since most cards carry a maximum liability of $50 if they are ever lost or stolen by an unauthorized person. Keeping cash on hand levels low can help to minimize your losses in the event someone targets you.

PAYING BILLS

Today, paying your bills is extremely easy with online options. Most companies will allow you to make payments through electronic fund transfers or EFTs. This is the same as writing a check but is done over the internet. In fact, you can often arrange for automatic payment so that your money is transferred on a specific schedule. This way you don't have to worry about missing a payment ever again.

MAKING A DEPOSIT

Depositing money is just as easy. Most employers and Social Security offer the option for direct deposits. Even dividends from stocks or annuities can be set up for direct deposit. If there is still the rare occasion that you get a physical check, you can cash or deposit it at any bank branch if you do your business with a nationwide chain.

If you do business with a smaller bank or a local credit union, you can always send checks for deposit in the mail. Just make sure you endorse them "For Deposit Only" and include a deposit slip if your bank requires it.

Balancing your account can be done through your bank's website if you have an online account set up with your bank. Most of these also have "real-time" online access so you can immediately see any deposits or payments the moment they occur. You can also view your current balance 24 hours a day from the website or your cell phone. You may still choose to get paper statements once a month, but this information will be out of date by the time you get it.

Modern banking methods have made maintaining your finances from the road a lot easier than conventional banking. There are so many online convenient things you can do from your RV. Another financial aspect that you need to keep in mind is your taxes.

Much of the legal system in the United States is designed around the premise that people are stationary in the place they live in. Aside from your social security number and driver's license, the most common piece of information you'll be asked for from authority, and government officials is your physical address.

RVers are required to declare a state as their primary residence. So when selecting the right state to call home, you should consider the tax options and benefits you may get. The first thing you want to consider is whether or not the state has an income tax. This will immediately give you a list of just nine states that don't have income tax:

1. Alaska

2. Florida

3. Nevada

4. New Hampshire

5. South Dakota

6. Tennessee

7. Texas

8. Washington

9. Wyoming

Of these states, Tennessee and New Hampshire do tax interest income and dividends, so they may not be the best for retired RV travelers. You'll also need to occasionally pass through your "home" state in order to renew vehicle registration, driver's license and other legal matters, so this often takes Alaska off the list as well.

The next step is to consider the sales tax. Most of the six remaining states aren't that different:

1. Wyoming - 4-8 percent

2. South Dakota - Over 4 percent

3. Washington - 6.5 percent

4. Texas - 6.25-8.25 percent

5. Nevada - 6.5-8.75 percent

6. Florida - Over 6 percent

Your property taxes won't be off too much concern unless you already live in one of these states and plan to keep your property as an income property while traveling around in your RV. However, the personal property tax will have an impact on your RV, car, and even household possessions. Nevada, South Dakota, Texas, and Wyoming do not have personal property taxes.

Using this information, it will make it easier for you to decide on which state to declare residency and save on your taxes at the same time.

ESTABLISHING RESIDENCY

Since you still need a residency for vehicle registration, voting, and health care, you need to establish a home state for your day to day tasks and paperwork. Let's look at what else you need to do for this.

DETERMINING STATE RESIDENCY

First, you need to understand how state residency works and what constitutes a state residency. Then you need to consider what the legal state residency requirements are. While officially being a resident of the state means living there, the residency laws vary greatly by state. Most states have a clause about living in a state for a specific amount of time before applying for state residency.

This is typically a year. However, that won't work if you want to live in an RV full-time and travel around the country of a foreign location. Luckily, there are other ways to fulfill state residency requirements for purposes of mail and taxes.

STATE RESIDENCY REQUIREMENTS

The easiest solution is to use the home address of a friend or relative who lives in the state. This can give you the address you need for a driver's license, mailing address, and vehicle registration. However, if you don't want to impose on them or don't have any friends, family, or acquaintances in your chosen state, then you need a different solution.

CHANGING STATE RESIDENCY

There are plenty of mail forwarding services that will set you up with a street address to help you officially establish residency. This means you can travel wherever you want and still have an official stable address. Just keep in mind that you will need to spend some time in the state in order to care for legal documents and paperwork associated with getting your residency established.

You will need to apply for a driver's license in person, and you may need to take the driver's test again. You must also register and ensure your vehicle in the state, but this can often be done over the phone or by mail. Voting laws will vary as well, so keep that in mind during the voting season. You can also acquire health insurance through the state.

Lastly, you'll be responsible for paying income taxes through the state of your residency.

LIVING IN AN RV FULL-TIME

A lot goes into living in an RV full-time. It is the same as living in a home; you have to cook your meals and keep up on your cleaning. However, living in an RV also comes with the added responsibility of maintenance and comfort. There are some things that just aren't the same as staying in a home and will require a little extra effort. Let's look at all the areas of RV living and how you can improve your experience.

MAKING YOUR RV MORE LIVABLE

The first step you need to take when living in an RV is to make the space more livable. You need to maximize your space because no matter what size your RV is and how little possessions you have, you'll still feel as if you don't have enough room. Since an RV only has so much space, what you choose to do with it will make the difference in terms of livable and comfortability. Let's look at some tips on how you can make your space cozier.

REDUCE POSSESSIONS

The first thing you want to do when living in an RV is to limit the number of things you keep in it. If you overload your space with too many items, then you will end up with a crowded RV that looks like it is unorganized, which is also dangerous (as we have already discussed). When deciding what to bring in your RV, consider the following:

- Take only the items you need and are going to use regularly.

- Take only items that have multiple uses.

- Never buy a new item without getting rid of an old one.

GET A WIDER RV

If you haven't already bought an RV or if you are thinking of trading in for a new one, the best way to increase living space if you need it is to buy a wide-body travel unit or one with more slide outs. The average RV width is 96 inches, but can sometimes go up to 102 inches. If you have an average 35 foot RV, this gives you an extra 17.5 feet of living space. The only difficulty is that these RVs are difficult to find.

In addition, if you buy an RV with slide rooms, you need to be aware of the fact that when in motion there isn't much interior space. When the slides are closed there is barely enough room for walking and certain areas of your RV can actually be inaccessible.

GET RID OF OVERSIZED FURNITURE

Most RV units come with multiple sofas and at least one oversized chair or a chair with an ottoman. If you eliminate this oversized furniture with a thin, sleek sofa or a smaller recliner chair without an ottoman, then you'll have more room and still won't be giving up your comfort.

RVs also have sleeper sofas that have built-in storage areas, so you have a place to put bulky items such as toilet paper, water bottles, and other things that take up a lot of room. Finding furniture with slide-out drawers rather than lift up seats is more convenient. You shouldn't replace an RV sofa with a household sofa since these won't have storage, are too deep, and can't be converted to beds when needed.

You can also make more room by replacing the eating booth with a table and chair set. This will allow you to have a bigger living area, but it will also reduce your storage space since most booths have built in areas under the seat to hold a variety of items. Booths can also convert to beds so you would lose this option by replacing them, which can be a problem if you plan on ever traveling with more than two people or playing host for a few nights. In a nutshell, it is up to you to decide which modifications are best for your individual situation.

CHOOSING HARD FLOORING

Most RVs used to come with plush and light-colored carpets, but most people found them difficult to keep clean. While they do provide some warmth in an RV, they also can make the unit seem smaller. Most people choose to remove the carpets and replace them with vinyl or laminate flooring that is easier to care for and allows the unit to appear larger. If you like the idea of carpeting, you can also choose to add lighter area rugs.

AVOID FANCY WINDOW COVERINGS

An RV can seem smaller if you have day/night shades, heavy curtains and thick valances. Replace them with thinner options like glossy aluminum mini blinds, as they will make the RV appear larger and more open while also being easier to care for.

CHOOSE FURNITURE WITH STORAGE

Sofas are only one of many furniture pieces that have built-in storage. You can find eating booths with this option as well. Even if these items take up more room, you can find them in thinner materials that will add a little more space and keep the area looking cleaner.

CHOOSE AN RV WITH BASEMENT STORAGE

You could also choose an RV that comes with an extra storage room beneath the main living area. This is where you can keep items such as tools, hoses, electrical wires, fishing gear, lawn chairs, cleaning products and pretty much any other bulky item that would otherwise take up too much square footage inside your RV. You can keep things organized in the basement through the use of crates and large plastic containers. You can also sometimes slide-out trays if your RV doesn't already have them.

SPACE SAVERS

Items you use in a home to organize your closets, drawers, and refrigerators will help to increase internal storage areas in your RV. Plastic containers can also help hold dry food products since they stack easily and avoid spilling of contents.

MAKE GOOD USE OF YOUR SPACE

You can easily become overwhelmed by the lack of living space in an RV, but you can avoid it by making good use of the feet you can work with the above tips. When you have a more liveable RV, you will be able to have a much more comfortable existence in your retirement. Now that we know how to make your space more liveable let's look at some cleaning tips so you can always keep your RV at its best and always have a comfortable and clean place to live.

Keeping your RV clean and sanitized is important for your health as well as your comfort. In addition, it also helps to maintain the value of your RV. When you live out of your RV, it is going to get dirty, and unless you maintain and clean it properly you will end up with an unsanitary environment. Avoid problems and discomfort with the following tips to help you keep your RV clean.

VACUUMING AND DUSTING

The best way to deal with dust in your RV is to vacuum and dust regularly. You have a couple of options:

- Shop-Vac

- Hand Vac

- Long Handled Duster

One or all of these can remove dust from the floors, windows, curtains, blinds, dashboards, upholstery, countertops, and inside the drawers and cabinets. Once you've vacuumed everything, you should wipe down the entire surface area with ammonia water or Windex in order to sanitize the area. This is important in the kitchen since it makes the area safe for food preparation.

CLEANING THE HOLDING TANKS

I'm not going to dive too deep into the details here, as I will discuss this in great detail in the repair and maintenance section. But I want to mention that germs can be unhealthy and even deadly. If you don't properly sanitize the holding tanks, then you will be increasing your chance of health problems as well as potential damage to your RV.

The sewer tank is the most important and requires the greatest amount of work since it can emit an extremely unpleasant, septic odor that spreads throughout the RV. It can also clog and cause other problems. Later we will talk about tank cleaning as well as the chemicals you should use for the process.

WINDOWS AND MIRRORS

If the windows in your RV aren't covered with a solar film, you can simply clean them with Windex. If you do have a solar film on your windows, you should follow the manufacturer's directions since some types can be damaged by specific cleaning products. Mirrors can often be cleaned just as you would at home. If you have any valances, vacuum them as you would the upholstery. Lastly, make sure you scrub both sides of the windows.

When it comes to cleaning curtains, shades and blinds, there is a little more work involved. Consider the following tips:

- If you have roll-up shades, they typically just need a good dusting.

  ☐ If your roll-up shades have a stain, you can wipe them with a damp cloth and some Windex.

- Other types of shades are best cleaned by hand dusting or a careful vacuuming.

- If your blinds are made from aluminum, then they are best cleaned by taking them down, laying them out on the ground and washing them with a mild detergent and a soft, light mop before hanging them up to dry.

    ☐ Shiny aluminum blinds often only need a light dusting since dirt typically doesn't cling to these types of blinds.

- Day-night shades tend to break easily so you should just vacuum them carefully.

    ☐ If they have a stain, you should wipe them with a damp cloth and Windex with Oxy. Allow them to dry then vacuum them gently.

- Blinds with water stains on them should be professionally cleaned.

UPHOLSTERY AND DASHBOARDS

Start by thoroughly vacuuming the dashboard area. Clean all surfaces with a leather or vinyl protector while remembering to clean the steering wheel and foot pedals.

If your furniture is leather, you can wipe it down with a damp cloth then with a leather or vinyl protector. If your furniture is fabric, vacuum it, spray it with Febreze, and keep a small blanket over it to protect it. At least once a year, you should consider having your fabric steam-cleaned.

CLEANING THE TOILET

A part of proper toilet maintenance is to use items specifically made for disinfecting the toilet and not damaging it. When cleaning an RV toilet, you should never use any of the following:

- Any kind of brush.

- Rags that aren't disposable.

- Rags with chemical residue from other cleaning areas.

You should ideally clean your RV toilet once a week and more often if you use it frequently. To properly clean it, you should use disposable paper towels, water, and a pine-based disinfecting cleaner such as Pine-Sol. Use the following steps to properly clean your toilet:

1. Add some water to the toilet bowl.

2. Pour the bottle's instructed amount of cleaner in the bowl.

3. Use paper towels to wipe down the bowl and upper rim.

4. Be sure to clean under the rim as well.

5. Partially open the flapper and wipe it down, be sure to get rid of any toilet paper or another residue.

6. Empty the contents.

7. Fill the bowl halfway with water and flush.

Ensure the bowl is clear of residue, if not then repeat the seven steps above again until the bowl is clean. Once you are done then move on to the second stage:

1. Add more water and cleaner to the bowl.

2. Use the paper towels and contents to wipe down the tops and bottoms of the seat as well as the sides and back of the entire toilet.

3. Flush the toilet and add more water.

4. Use some clean towels to wipe down everything you just cleaned in order to get rid of any sticky residue.

5. Spray down the entire toilet with Lysol.

6. Dry the exterior of the toilet, and you are completely cleaned and sanitized.

As you can tell, there isn't much in the way of equipment and/or chemicals to clean your toilet. However, you need to do things properly in order to sanitize appropriately. If you clean the outside of the toilet before the bowl, then you are transferring germs and dirt into an area you are trying to sanitize. By cleaning the bowl first, you can sue it as a bucket, and it will make completing the process easier. Don't forget to wear rubber gloves to protect your hands from any unwanted bacteria.

CLEANING THE BATHROOM

Most RV shower stalls and tubs are made from heavy plastic. This means they will scratch easily. If the surface is scratched, dirt can build up on the floors and walls, causing these to get ruined. The same can happen if you use the wrong cleaning products. There are two ways you can keep your shower or tub clean:

1. Wipe them down with a dry towel or squeegee after each use. Use Windex with Ammonia to clean any glass and metal surfaces.

2. Use a spray such as Clean Shower after each use.

Either one of these methods uses gentle cleaning products that will keep your shower and tub clean without ruining the textures.

For the other areas of your bathroom, clean in the following way:

1. Use Windex with ammonia and paper towels to spray and wipe down glass, mirrors, countertops, sinks and the exterior of any cabinets.

2. Use Lysol to spray down sinks, toilets, and countertops when finished.

3. Mop or wipe down the floor with an ammonia-based product, ammonia water, or a pine based deodorizing cleaner.

CLEANING THE FLOORS

It can be hard to keep the floors of your RV clean, but using the following tips it can make the process a lot easier:

- Vinyl or ceramic tile floors can be cleaned with ammonia or ammonia and water.

- For laminate flooring, you should dry mop first and then lightly mist and mop with a mix of ¼ cup vinegar to one gallon of water. It is also best to use a microfiber floor mop.

- If you have carpets, they should be steam-cleaned and vacuumed frequently.

  ☐ You can choose to cover them with clear plastic backed runners if you want to reduce the amount of cleaning.

Keeping your RV clean and sanitized will make it more livable and far healthier for you and everyone else residing there. Living in your RV is meant to be pleasant and enjoyable, giving you time for the things you want to do. While cleaning isn't fun, it is absolutely necessary, and doing proper cleaning and maintenance updates will make the process quicker and easier. Another thing you'll need to focus on in an RV is how to keep your pests under control.

KEEPING PESTS UNDER CONTROL

Traveling by RV is a great way to explore the wonderful outdoors. However, you won't want the outdoors to come inside your RV in the form of pests. Let's consider some tips and strategies that can help you keep pests out of your RV.

Fleas, ticks and other blood-sucking insects are the worst types of pests you can bring into your RV. This is especially true in the sense of ticks that carry Lyme disease in some parts of the country. The main way these form of pests get into the RV is by hitching a ride on you, your supplies, and your pets if you are traveling with them. There are three ways you can avoid bringing these pests into your RV.

Avoid Having Them Attach to You

If you have pets and you take them out for a hike, be sure they have a tick collar or monthly tick prevention. This is the best way to protect your pets, and it isn't going to pollute the environment. You can also apply a spray or special essential oils to your legs and pants as a precaution against having them attach to you and your clothing.

While hiking you can also avoid tall grass, underbrush, and shaded areas under trees to avoid exposure. Ticks will attach to you when you brush through their nests, and most of these are hidden and shaded from direct sunlight. You will reduce your risk of exposure by staying on trails and in open terrain.

Remove Them When You Return

After you travel through any potential area for ticks, do a pest check before getting in your RV. Check everywhere that can be infested. This means brushing off your pant legs, socks and shoes. If you are wearing shorts, then check your legs. Shake out and brush off camping gear that was in contact with the ground, particularly blankets and chairs. Also, check your pets thoroughly for anything crawling in their fur.

Contain the Pests

In case you miss any pests, consider changing out of your hiking clothes as soon as you get into your trailer. Place the clothes in a secure laundry container and keep them there until they can be washed. This is especially important with pants and socks.

You won't need to worry about other clothing unless they come into contact with potential tick hiding places. This is also a good time to take a shower. If you notice your pet scratching or chewing more than usual, you should do a thorough check and get rid of any pests you find with a pet spray, balm, or oil.

LIMIT FOOD EXPOSURE

Pests come into your RV for two reasons: food and shelter. There isn't much you can do for the shelter portion of it unless you like to live in the cold. However, there is plenty you can do to prevent your RV from becoming a food buffet for bugs, rodents, and other critters. Consider the following tips to help in this area.

Stay Clean. After each time you cook to be sure you clean completely. This even means getting rid of the grease on the walls of your kitchen. All dishes should be cleaned right away, and you should keep down the number of crumbs and other debris as well.

Avoid Leaving Food Out. Make sure all food is sealed in plastic or metal containers. Cardboard boxes generally don't give enough protection since mice will chew them up for nesting material and will get to the food before other insects and pests. Keep in mind your pet food as well, so don't keep pet food out at all times. An excellent way to keep your pet food safe and away from any humidity is to store it in a large plastic, sealed container with a lid.

Seal Your Garbage. Pests are perfectly content to eat your leftovers. So make sure you keep your garbage in a well-sealed container too.

Reduce Scents. Most pests are attracted to garbage and food by scent. Use scents they don't prefer in your galley near the garbage in order to deter insects to some extent. A few of these involve citronella, lavender, and vinegar.

REDUCE OPENINGS IN YOUR RV

It should be obvious that the fewer openings you have in your RV, the less chance critters will be able to get inside your RV. Make sure your doors and windows have good screens so you can get a supply of fresh air without having to worry about insects and critters getting inside.

You'll also want to check the underside of your RV for any potential points of entry for critters. This is particularly important if you own an older RV. There may be openings on the underside that you can't see at first. You don't want critters getting into the floor or walls of your trailer. Seal up any openings you find.

One insect you should be aware of if you own an RV is the mud dauber. This is a type of wasp that is known for making its home in RVs. They are typically attracted to the exhaust that comes from RV refrigerators. If you find these insects to be a problem in your area, be sure to put screens on your exhaust ports.

Lastly, avoid leaving your sewage hose open and connected. When not in use, keep your sewer hose off or completely closed. Cockroaches can get into your black tank through the hose, and from there they can get into the rest of your trailer. This is nearly impossible for them to do if you only have the hose open while draining.

GET A GUARD DOG

For years, dogs and cats have helped control pests. Just the scent and presence of these animals will deter some pests, and in some cases, they will actively hunt critters. While pets can be a vector for insects getting into the RV, there are some pets that can be effective guardians for your RV.

RESPOND IMMEDIATELY

If you do find unwanted insects or critters in your RV, then you want to respond immediately. Try to use environmentally-friendly insect-repelling products. If you must use poison or insecticide, try to choose one that doesn't poison a whole colony, since you only want to get rid of what is in your RV.

Also, be extremely careful with poisons and insecticides since they are often harmful to humans and pets if they are inhaled or if something you eat came in contact with them. If you need something to kill pests instantly, be sure you dispose of them in the garbage. Don't allow the poison to get into the wild and risk making other animals sick.

If you need to do full fumigation, then you should wait until you aren't in the wilderness and once you have another place to sleep in for the next few days, as the experience will be toxic.

Preparing meals in an RV can be challenging, but there are things you can do to make it easier. A lot of what makes cooking in an RV easier has to do with your attitude. If you plan to do a lot of baking from scratch and you are going to spend the majority of your time in the kitchen, then it can be a little more challenging. Let's look at how cooking here is different from cooking in a home and how you can improve your cooking experience in an RV.

Cooking in an RV is a challenge that requires you to make some adjustments to how you cook. However, once you do this, it will be a lot easier to prepare food. The galley of an RV is far different from that of a standard kitchen since the ovens, refrigerators, and pantries are smaller.

Plus you will have more limited counter space and storage areas. If you use propane for cooking, you'll also need to adjust your timing since gas often burns hotter than electric. Until you learn to work with these differences, you will be slightly limited in the meals you prepare in your RV.

CAREFULLY STOCK YOUR GALLEY

Since your RV galley doesn't have much room, you need to choose carefully when stocking it. Consider the following tips to help:

- A small freezer won't store too much-frozen food.

- Large bottles of milk and soda not only take up refrigerator space but also may not fit on refrigerator shelves.

- Refrigerator bins won't fit bulky vegetables.

- Small items are more likely to slide off the kitchen and refrigerator shelves while the RV is in motion.

- Fresh fruit will spoil before it can be eaten if you purchase it in large quantities.

- Liquid items can spill.

Plastic containers are key to protecting food and making storage easier. They come in a range of sizes, are unbreakable, and can be stacked for convenient storage.

Don't Use Propane

Cooking and baking with propane will end up in you wasting a lot of money. With the cost of propane, it will cost an average of $3.50 an hour to cook with it. If you have a propane generator, then you'll be spending even more. If possible, use electric cookware while hooked up to electricity.

If you are in a park, sometimes your camping fees will even include the cost of electricity. Any food that you cook on a stove or in an oven can be cooked in an electric appliance for the most part. If you prefer to cook on a stove, then consider getting a portable electric burner, which can also work beautifully for outdoor cooking.

11 Useable Tips & Tricks to Plan Your Meal Carefully

It is also a good idea to plan ways to create easy, healthy, and tasteful meals. It can be helpful to have a range of powdered, canned, frozen and instant foods. Perhaps the most important thing is to plan your meals in advance. If you plan to stay in one place for a while, crock pot meals are an excellent option.

Although challenging, you can even cook this way while the RV is moving. Most RVers choose to use the microwave or electric frying pan. Consider some of the following tips to help with easier food and beverage preparation:

1. Use a coffee pot to heat water then use the hot water to make hot drinks, iced tea, instant oatmeal, mashed potatoes, soups or other foods that require it. You can fill and heat the water, then use it whenever you need a hot drink or food. This saves not only time but also money since you won't need to run a generator.

2. Remove meat from the freezer in the morning so it can be thawed in time for cooking dinner. Keep a few frozen meals on hand for fast meals on the days you spend long hours driving.

3. Keep nonfat dry milk on hand for when you need to make items that require milk.

4. Choose meats that can thaw quickly, such as shrink-wrapped ham slices.

5. Consider buying your baked goods rather than making them since it will be cheaper, cleaner and easier. Plus, you get to have a taste of local bread and artisanal creations.

6. Limit your supply of fresh fruits and vegetables while keeping frozen or canned on hand so you can quickly make side dishes and desserts.

7. Dinner leftovers can be kept for lunch the next day.

8. Bread and cakes can be stored in the oven to save counter and refrigerator space while helping the foods stay moist.

9. Keeping a supply of cheese and crackers on hand is great for the light snack when you aren't very hungry or don't have time to prepare a meal.

10. If possible, you should avoid grills since they are bulky and can be difficult to clean. Instead, consider ordering them in restaurants for the occasional treat and break from your RV.

11. Try to use paper plates and plastic utensils as often as possible, particularly on travel days. This saves time on cleanup and makes it easier to get on the road.

Cooking in an RV doesn't have to be that difficult with a little preparation and planning. The above tips help in the cooking and food selection process. However, if you still want to use the oven, there are some additional tips you need to consider. As with stove cooking, you'll need to make a few adjustments and learn how the oven in your specific RV works before you can have a delicious, baked meal or treat.

Remember the Small Size. Your RV oven is going to be smaller than the one you are used to in your home. This means you will likely need smaller baking pans. Also, keep in mind that you won't be able to roast a whole chicken while baking a tray of vegetables. So make sure you plan and adjust accordingly. Measure the inside of your oven in advance and ensure your baking pans will fit.

Monitor Your Temperature. You should never rely on the temperature dial of your oven; it often isn't accurate. Use an oven safe thermometer inside your oven to be safe and always monitor the temperature. After a few times, you'll start to realize how off your dial is and then you can start adjusting accordingly.

Completely Pre-Heat. The biggest drawback to an RV oven is that it won't alert you when it reaches the right temperature. However, you will still need to pre-heat it. The best way to do this is to check the oven thermometer every five to ten minutes until it reaches the desired temperature.

Soon you'll get an idea of how long the pre-heat process takes, then you'll be able to set a timer and start cooking when it sounds off. Most RV ovens take longer to preheat than you think, sometimes up to 20 minutes. While this may seem like you are wasting propane and money, most RV ovens cook in less time so it will likely even out in the end.

Get Even Heat with a Baking Stone. Perhaps the biggest issue people face with oven cooking in an RV is the fact that food tends to burn on the bottom. Consider how the RV oven works: it is heated by a flame that comes from a metal rod inside the oven. On top of the flame is a metal shelf that distributes heat.

However, the metal plate doesn't do this well all the time, and as a result, you are left with a hot spot on top of the flame and cool spots away from the flame. A baking stone or unglazed tiles on top of the metal shelf can help solve this problem. The stone or tiles will serve as an insulator from the flame and will absorb or distribute the heat throughout the oven. Just ensure that when placing the stone or tiles you aren't blocking the ventilation holes on the sides of the shelf and that they are clean.

Adjust the Placement of Your Metal Rack. Most RV ovens only have one rack inside. However, this doesn't mean it needs to be in a fixed position. Typically they have three levels where you can place the rack. It is best to keep it in the middle, but you can adjust if you need more or less heat.

Remember to Rotate. Once you've preheated your oven, adjusted your rack, and placed your heating stone, there is one last thing you need to remember. Set a timer and remember to rotate your food halfway through the cooking process to ensure you get even cooking.

This may seem like a lot of work, but doing so will make it easier to prepare food and cook in your RV. This will go a long way to making it more liveable as well. Now, in the case of both the stove and the oven, it is always a great tip to skip turning either of them on while you are near a historic town or city, and instead attend the farmer's markets. This way you get fresh, handmade snacks and meals as you also experience the local culture and produce of that location.

DUMPING AND CLEANING THE SEWER TANK IN 5 EASY STEPS

When we talked about cleaning your RV, we mentioned the waste water tank. Dumping and cleaning the waste water tank is one of those things that can be included under cleaning and sanitizing, as a part of living in your RV, and lastly as a part of the regular maintenance and upkeep of your RV. So let's look at the important task of dumping and cleaning your sewer tank.

Without a clean and sanitized sewer tank, not only will your RV smell like an unkept public toilet, but you'll also be breeding bacteria. You may also risk clogging your plumbing system which requires a whole other level of work and potentially expensive repairs.

However, don't be afraid; cleaning the sewer tank isn't an unmanageable task and doesn't take a lot of time. In fact, with the following tips, you will be able to keep your plumbing system functioning, your RV smelling fresh and soapy, and you won't even need to get your hands dirty.

#1 - SELF PROTECTION

The stuff coming from your sewer hose is toxic, so you'll need to protect both yourself and your clothing. To do this, wear rubber gloves, shoe covers, and protective glasses as well as something to cover your mouth and nose like a bandanna or a scarf. You should also keep some paper towels and liquid soap outside to wash your hands, gloves, and shoe coverings at an outside faucet before heading back into your RV.

#2 - PREPARATION

You will obviously need to be parked beside a sewer outlet to dump. This can be at either your campsite or at a dumping station. If you are at a dump station, you'll connect your sewer hose to the RV and place the other end into the sewer opening. If you are staying at a full hookup campsite, your hose is likely to be connected to a sewer outlet.

If your RV is stationary, keep your waste water tank valve closed and your gray water valve open. Before you dump, you'll want to close your gray water valve and fill it halfway with soap.

#3 - EMPTY YOUR TANKS

You should always empty your tanks before they are full since too much liquid is heavy and will damage the tanks. Remember that a gallon of water weighs over eight pounds. So the average RV tank of 45 gallons will add about 375 pounds when full, and this can cause problems.

Avoid issues by dumping when your tank is no more than half full. This also helps you to clean and sanitize your tanks more often, which in turn avoids clogs. Let's look at the steps involved in emptying your RV tanks:

1. Once you are hooked up and ready to dump, open the sewer tank valve. After the waste matter is gone from the tank, close the sewer valve. Run fresh water into the tank, pull the valve and dump the contents a second time.

a. Consider using a clear hose adapter to help you see what is coming out of the tank.

2. Keep filling and dumping your tank until you see the water running clear.

3. Once the water is running clear, close the wastewater valve and open the grey water valve.

4. Allow the contents to empty into the sewer outlet. This will clean the interior part of the connector hose and keep the matter from getting stuck.

If you are going to stay in place, then keep the black water valve closed and add a gallon of water. You can also add some Spic N Span to the tank. Keep the gray water valve open.

If you are going to hit the road in your RV, close both valves and place an enzyme cleaner along with a gallon of water into the sewer tank. As you drive the mixture will slosh in the tank and break up hardened matter while disinfecting the tank. This will help reduce clogs and any odors that may infiltrate your RV.

#4 - DEEP CLEAN THE TANK

First-time RVers tend to think that emptying the sewer tanks is enough to keep them clean and to smell good, but there is more to it. When using your RV for a living, you need to dump the tanks every few days and deep clean at least once a week.

To deep clean your RV sewer tank, you need to do the following steps:

1. Fill the tank ¾ full with fresh water and two cups of bleach.

2. Close the toilet lid to avoid toxic fumes.

3. Allow it to sit for 10 minutes, no longer.

4. Drain the sewer tank.

5. Fill the tank with fresh water and drain immediately.

Continue this process until you see that the clear hose connector has no debris and there is no more bleach smell. This is important because if there is any bleach left behind it can damage the plumbing system.

#5 - BACKWASH THE SEWER TANK

The last step you need to take is to backwash the tank. This requires you to use pressurized water to push against the interior walls and floor of the tank to loosen and flush out any hardened matter. You can do this in one of two ways.

1. Use a built-in system that comes with your RV.

2. Use hand-held equipment that connects to your hose.

Let's look a little closer at both of these methods.

#1 - Built-In System. Simply connect a green garden hose to the system connection on your RV then turn on the pressure washing valve on the RV. Keep the water running until you see clear water running through the clear hose adapter.

#2 - Using a Hand-Held Wand. Attach a green garden hose to the water spigot at your site. Connect the backwash wand to the hose. Pull the wand and hose through a window or the door of the RV into the bathroom. Open the flapper of the toilet and place the wand down the opening. Have someone outside to turn the water on for you and keep moving the wand back and forth until the helper outside sees the waste is running clear.

ENZYME TREATMENTS

After your sewer tank is dumped and cleaned, you can treat it with biologically-friendly enzyme treatment. Depending on the size of your RV tank, you may dump every three to five days; so you likely won't add this product each day. Although adding this product occasionally will make it easier to clean in the future and will help keep your tank smelling better. Simply add a packet to your tank and add a gallon of water.

The enzymes work to eat away at the sludge that has accumulated in the tank along the walls and bottom. By softening this material, it will flow from your plumbing system when you clean next. Without this, the clumps can break off and clog your system. This can lead to costly repairs.

Following the guidelines above will help keep your tank clean, sanitized, and smelling great. It may seem like a lot of work, but it will save you a lot of headaches later.

ALL SEASON COMFORTABILITY

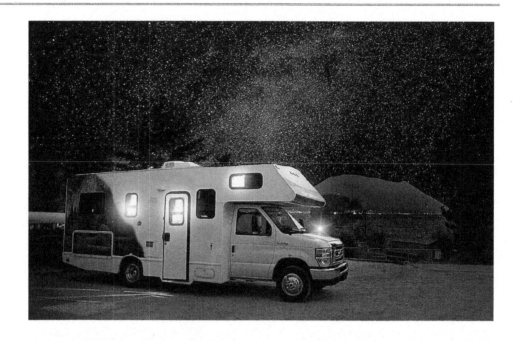

WAYS TO STAY COOL IN THE SUMMER

Most RVs come with all the basic comfort systems, but there may be times they aren't operating at their best or they aren't enough in extreme weather. With some precautions, you can keep your RV comfortable and liveable in the hot summer months. In the summer months, an RV can become quite warm when sitting out in the sun. There are a few things you can do to keep yourself cool and comfortable. No matter what type of RV you have, the following tips can help you.

KNOW THE BASICS

There are some basic rules of nature you need to keep in mind when trying to keep your RV cool in the summer. Consider the following basic five facts:

1. The night is cooler than the day.

2. The sun rises in the east and sets in the west.

3. The shade is cooler than direct sunlight.

4. Moving air cools while still, air is hot and sticky.

5. Cold air drops and hot air rises.

Because of these five facts, it is clear that the orientation of your RV is the first thing to take in mind. Parking your RV with respect to the sun will dramatically affect temperatures inside your RV. Parking beside a shaded tree can reduce the effects of the sun, but also parking, so the sun shines on the side with the least windows.

SHADE IS YOUR FRIEND

The temperature in the shade is often five or more degrees cooler than in direct sunlight. If you are checking into a campsite in the summer, ask if there is a site available in the shade. Remember that if your RV is dark in color, it will absorb more heat than a lighter colored RV.

Windows and Awnings

After setting up your RV, open all of the window awnings. These awnings will provide shade over the windows and cool the air around the immediate exterior of the vehicle. You should also try to choose a site that allows you largest awning to be on either the east or west side of the RV, depending on the time of the day when you plan to be outside the most. If you are going to be out more in the morning, the awning should be facing east and the opposite if you are out more in the evening.

Sunscreens

Some RV have awnings with built-in sunscreens at the outer edges. These sunscreens can help when your RV is out in the afternoon sun. If you have these, you should utilize them and if your RV doesn't have them then consider installing them if you are going to be staying somewhere warm in the summer.

Tarps

Be sure to always have extra tarps on hand. If needed, you can stretch an extra tarp over your campsite for added shade.

Umbrellas

Lastly, you can use big beach umbrellas if you have them. The umbrella will often give you at least a little bit of shade and a spot to sit outside.

CIRCULATE THE AIR

If your air conditioner isn't doing well enough to cool your RV, open the windows on the shady side of the RV and keep the windows closed on the side that is in direct sunlight. This causes natural air circulation.

Another way to get air circulation is to have the RV in a position where you can pull in cool air with the ceiling fan instead of hot air. The biggest mistake that RV owners make is to place their RV in a hot place and then push that hot air into the RV by turning on ceiling fans.

Just make sure you close the shades on the sunny side of the RV in order to block out the sun. You may even want to consider putting a reflector in the windows that are facing the sun.

EFFECTIVE AIR CONDITIONER USE

Modern RVs have at least one air conditioning unit. With a little planning and care, you can use this unit to maximum efficiency while reducing your power consumption. If you are using shade, window screens and awnings as we've already discussed previously, you probably won't even need to use your air conditioning. However, there may come a time when you need to use your air conditioner to cool the inside of the RV.

Don't turn the air conditioner on inside your RV until the internal temperature is about 75 degrees Fahrenheit. At this point, close all the windows and turn on the air conditioner while leaving the ceiling fan on as well. This allows the fan to pull out hot air at the ceiling and reduce the air conditioning load.

If the temperature is 85 degrees or higher inside and the air conditioner isn't bringing the temperature down, you should consider turning off the air conditioner and open the windows for increased air circulation.

Before dusk, the temperature outside will start dropping. While it will still be hot, it will be cooler than the midday hours. This is the time to turn off your air conditioning, open the windows, turn the ceiling fan on high and pull the cooler evening air into the RV. After the temperature has dropped enough, you can turn the air conditioner back on if needed. This will help you save on energy usage.

MAKE YOUR MEALS OUTSIDE

With proper planning, you can prepare and cook a lot of meals outside. This will reduce the temperature inside your RV. You can cook outside with a grill, electric frying pan, electric broiler, crock pot or anything similar. You will need to buy groceries accordingly and plan your meals as needed.

Another option is to cook enough for a few days on a cooler day. Then on a hotter day, you can make up with the leftovers; this takes less time and heat. Alternatively, you could also just eat out at a restaurant or marketplace.

Balmy, humid weather typically makes us crave a nice cold slice of juicy watermelon, pasta or vegetable salad, or perhaps a nice chicken quesadilla with a glass of beer or lemonade. Essentially, eating cooler foods not only saves cooking time and energy, but it also keeps you refreshed.

GET OUTSIDE TO BEAT THE HEAT

The heat of the day often stretches from about eleven in the morning to an hour before sunset. One way you can stay cool is to plan your daily activities to take you away from the RV during this time. Consider seeing the sights, doing some outdoor activities or just doing your shopping, so you aren't inside when it is hot. Remember to ALWAYS take your pet with you if you are exiting the RV during a hot day. Never, ever leave them indoors, regardless of whether the windows are open or not.

Doing these things will help you stay cool in the summer. But what if you find yourself staying in your RV when the cold of winter sets in? Let's look at that next.

WAYS TO KEEP WARM IN THE WINTER

Just because the weather cools down, it doesn't mean you can't live comfortably in your RV. While most live in an RV so they can travel with the weather and go where the climate is comfortable in the winter, you may still find yourself spending a few days in a cold location, or you may want to vacation somewhere cooler.

No matter the reason you find yourself living in the cold for a while, the following tips will help you stay warm in your RV. The first thing you need to do is prepare your vehicle.

7 MUST FOLLOW STEPS TO PREPARE THE RV FOR WINTER

The first step you need to take is to make sure the exterior of your RV is prepared to handle the cold of winter.

Check all the window seals and apply caulking as needed. Keep cold drafts out by checking all the weather stripping and replace anything if needed. Cut some foam boards for insulation and place them between your RV frame and the ground. If needed, consider getting an RV skirt to avoid drafts underneath.

HOLDING TANKS

Empty both your gray and black water tanks before the weather gets too cold or before you head into the colder climate. Add pink antifreeze to both tanks to protect the dump valves from freezing. Consider using foam pipe insulation to protect the pipes or if you plan to camp in the cold for an extended period of time, consider electric pipe heaters. Insulate your sewer hose and prevent ice dams by using heat tape. If needed, add a holding tank heater.

WATER PUMP

Keep your water pump from freezing with a small space heater.

WINDOWS

If needed, upgrade to dual pane windows for your RV. Keep the interior warm with insulated curtains. You can also use insulated curtains to separate the living area from the driving area, so you have less cabin area to heat. It can also help save money on electricity and propane usage. Another tip is to cover your windows with foam-backed insulation.

CEILING VENTS

Heat can leak out of skylights and roof vents. Use RV vent cushions to seal these; they fit over most standard-sized vents.

REFRIGERATOR

If the outside temperature drops below zero, then the refrigerant in the refrigerator will turn into a gel that clogs the coil system in the refrigerator. You can prevent this by removing the outside refrigerator access cover and putting duct tape over the two or three vent slots.

FURNACE

The furnace is what keeps you warm, so it would be rather proper if you were to test it before heading into a cold climate. Ensure it is cleaned by removing all insects, debris, and dust with a soft brush or compressed air.

If there isn't a furnace in your RV, buy heat fins or a heat pump. You may also want to consider an extra heat source, especially if the temperature outside is going to be below 40 degrees Fahrenheit.

ENGINE BLOCK HEATER

This is a great option if you are living in an extremely cold area. Just remember you need to turn it on for three hours before starting your engine.

HOW TO STAY WARM INSIDE

Once you have winterized and prepared your RV for the colder climates, there are a few more things you can do inside your RV to help keep your warm and comfortable.

INTERIOR DRAFTS

After you've sealed up all entry points for drafts on the outside, check for air leaks on the inside. If you find a spot where cool air is coming inside, there are a few ways you can fix the leak.

Insulated "Snakes." These can be easily found in most department stores and are often used to place along the bottom of doors in your house to prevent cold air from entering. They also work well for plugging small spaces under the doors of RVs.

Painter's Tape. Found at your local hardware store, this option can be used to seal small spots behind cabinets or appliances. It can easily be removed later with no residue left behind.

INSULATE WITH CURTAINS, WINDOW SHADES, AND RUGS

Any shades need to stay close to help keep drafts out of the RV. Even if you have double pane windows, keeping the shades closed will give an added layer of air between the window and the insulation of the interior of the RV.

Put throw rugs in the central areas of your RV where you walk most often. This will protect your feet from the cold and uninsulated floors.

USING THE FURNACE

First, you must read the manual, so you perform all required maintenance at regular times. Also, be realistic about the temperature setting of your furnace. Run the furnace mostly in the morning to heat up the interior. Turn it off or down once you are comfortable or won't be inside the RV; this will reduce the cost of propane needed to operate the furnace, and will also reduce noise.

Heat Pumps

The air conditioner on your RV roof may be a heat-pump type, which means it can do both heating and cooling; this can save you a lot of money if used strategically. The heat pump works well down to 40 degrees Fahrenheit, which can be more convenient than using a propane-based furnace.

Dress Warm

A more obvious suggestion but still worthwhile mentioning: dress warmly to help stand against the cold climate. Dressing appropriately can dramatically improve your comfort.

- Have a warm pair of sweatpants and a sweatshirt for when you are inside the RV.

- Wear thick socks when inside, as this will keep your feet warm and protect them from drafts.

- A pair of slippers can add an extra layer of warmth.

- Wear comfortable pajamas to stay warm at night.

Electric Blanket

If you are in a cold climate, the electric blanket may be your favorite accessory. It is best to keep your furnace low at night when you are under the comfort and warmth of the blankets, and this can be even better with an electric blanket. If you can get a dual-control blanket, you will also save on both electricity and propane.

CERAMIC ELECTRIC SPACE HEATERS

Another good purchase option is a ceramic space heater. This can help increase the temperature inside your RV a little from that provided by the propane furnace. It is cheap to operate and provides a steady source of heat throughout the day. You can also move it from the living area in the day to the bedroom at night. When choosing a space heater make sure it has the following requirements:

- A small footprint since storage space is limited.

- A ceramic heater has a better safety record than open-element types.

- A built-in sensor to turn off automatically if it is knocked over.

- A multi-speed fan allowing you to adjust how much heat is put out.

- A removable filter to clean any dust or dirt that clogs the unit.

The cold, as with heat, is livable if you do a little bit of preparation and make a few changes. The goal of living in your RV is to be comfortable year-round, and you can do this with the tips we've just discussed. At the end of the day, there are few things more comforting than curling up beside a loved one under a nest of blankets while holding a steaming cup of instant hot chocolate, and reading or talking about any subject you desire.

Being part of the mobile life implies certain safety procedures must be discussed and employed in your daily experiences as to avoid any accidents of any sort.

Beyond the basics of knowing safety while walking outdoors at a campground or keeping your possessions inside your RV, you need to pay attention to factors like driving safety, fire safety and being prepared with a plan in case of a natural disaster.

There are plenty of dangers that can happen when you are living in an RV, and you can reduce your risk of being a victim of any of them with a little extra reviewing and information. So let's take a look at everything you can do to stay safe in any type of condition.

Driving Safety

As we already discussed at the beginning of this book, when you are new to an RV your first step is to learn how to drive safely. By this point, I am assuming you already have or intend to practice often, so much so that you are now used to the mechanics of your vehicle. Whenever you are on the road, you practice safe driving techniques and are always aware of your surroundings.

You can avoid the majority of mishaps by driving within the posted speed limit, being mindful while entering or exiting highways, being careful when pulling into fuel stops, and avoiding distractions while the RV is in motion. However, even if you do all these things you still have to worry about the drivers around you who may not be as safe and careful as you.

If you remain alert at all times, you can avoid dangerous drivers around you. If you notice someone who is driving unsafe, stay as far away as you can. This may slow the time it takes you to reach your destination, but at least you'll get there safe and sound.

Maintain Your Vehicles

While it may be costly and time-consuming to repair and maintain your vehicle, it can be safer if you prevent your RV from falling into disrepair. An RV that is in disrepair won't be safe to drive. Later we are going to discuss how you can make minor repairs on your own and how to check regularly for problems; this will help reduce some of the costs involved. Regular safety checks can ensure everything is safe and in working order to avoid problems.

PROTECT YOUR POSSESSIONS

Most people feel they are safe in a campground or RV park, but this isn't always the case. Most of these areas have poor security, so you need to take precautions to protect your possessions.

- Never leave equipment or gear outside when you are off to do activities.

- If you have valuables, consider installing a safe in your RV.

- If needed, take small valuables with you when you are away from the RV.

- Consider changing and getting new locks for your RV to make it more secure.

- Place dowels in the window track to secure windows.

- Lock all windows and doors when you leave.

Always assume that stopping areas aren't as safe as they ought to be. Make it a point to never leave your doors and windows open, never allow strangers to enter your RV, and never go outside after dark. Choose your site carefully to avoid getting one that is near to insect homes or one that isn't leveled. You may also want to test the water before ingesting it.

By always being aware of your surroundings and using basic common sense you will be able to stay safe no matter where you are. The same applies to dry camping in the wilderness particularly with dangers such as toxins, animals, insects, and water to consider. In addition, you want to be properly prepared for emergencies since your cell phone may not work and you may be far away from help. In the end, it is important that you don't stay anywhere you can't feel safe and avoid taking any unnecessary risks.

When you live in an RV, there is nothing other than three inches of the wall protecting you. This is why you should use the following safe camping practices:

- Only stay overnight in locations that are well-populated and monitored regularly.

- Hide any cash or valuables.

- If you don't feel safe, leave and go somewhere else.

- Don't go outside to investigate noises at night, call the campground manager or 911 instead.

- If you plan to carry a gun, make sure it is legal, and you know how to use it.

- Keep your windows covered when inside.

Protecting Your Health

Always make sure you have plenty of your medications, supplements, and vitamins on hand and ensure you have a well-stocked and up-to-date first-aid kit at all times. With proper preparation and basic first-aid knowledge, you can likely save yourself a trip to the hospital or give yourself the extra time needed to make it to one.

Understand Nature

Nature is both beautiful and wonderful, but also deadly. You may choose a place for its peaceful and quiet beauty, but it also has risks, especially if you aren't used to living in the great outdoors. Therefore, read up and train yourself for outdoor living and practice a sharp sense of vigilance.

Be Prepared

One of the best and easiest ways to stay safe while living in an RV is to prepare yourself for as many potential problems as possible. This means doing a system and mechanical check of your RV regularly, carrying the right equipment to help in the event of problems, and being alert and vigilant to your surroundings.

HAVE AN ESCAPE PLAN

Lastly, you want to make sure you always have an escape plan. Remember three things can happen in an RV:

1. They collapse quickly in front end accidents.

2. They roll over easily due to a high center of gravity.

3. They are extremely flammable.

If any of these three things happened, do you know what you would do? Most people don't think about this, which is why it is important to have an escape plan in place and practice it regularly so you'll know what to do in an emergency situation.

As a part of that practice, you want to know where exit windows are in your RV and how to use them. Have a plan of action in case you need to get out quickly.

DEALING WITH SEVERE WEATHER IN AN RV

While you can plan and prepare for a lot of things in your RV, one thing you can't really plan for is severe weather. When you're out on the road, it is only a matter of time before you run into severe weather such as thunderstorms, hail, or even tornadoes.

Anything can happen at any time and place; the worst storms can come and go in a matter of an hour or two. The best thing you can do when it comes to severe weather is to know exactly how to handle yourself in any scenario.

BE INFORMED

Even the worst storm is going to have at least a few hours' notice. Thanks to modern radars and weather tracking, it is unlikely that you'll be surprised by severe weather. With an internet connection or a smartphone, you can check weather websites or use an app to see what the weather holds for the day. If you see signs of an approaching storm or there is a warning of harsh conditions, then start making plans for how to deal with it.

PLAN AND PREPARE

If you are planning to stay put during a storm, bring everything inside the vehicle and roll up your awnings to prevent any damage.

PACK AN EMERGENCY BAG

Should you have to leave your RV due to severe weather, you likely won't have much time to gather your belongings. Instead, you should always have an emergency bag on hand

and be ready to go at a moment's notice. While it is easy to think you can simply take your RV with you, this may not always be the case.

The emergency bag should have any important documents you need, enough medication for a few days, a few bottles of water, non-perishable food, cell phone chargers, and anything else you may need to live with during that period of time.

KNOW WHERE TO GO

RVs provide a certain degree of protection from the elements, but in a severe weather situation, you will need to seek shelter in a more stable and secure location. If you are staying at an RV park make sure you find the location of the nearest storm shelter and have a plan in place on how you'll get there if a warning is issued.

KNOW THE EVACUATION ROUTES

There is a range of conditions that can require people to evacuate an area at a moment's notice. If you arrive somewhere whether it be for a night or longer, make sure you know the evacuation routes for the area.

KNOW WHERE TO PARK

Depending on the severe weather, you may also want to keep an eye out for a place to park that is out of the way. For example, if a tornado is in the vicinity, you may want to pull over and find a secure place to park.

You should avoid parking under bridges or overpasses since you will be in the path of debris as well as causing traffic to back up. After getting parked you should get as low as you can in the vehicle; at least under the windows and cover your head with a blanket or a jacket.

GET TO A LOWER AREA

If you can get to the ground that is lower than the roadway you should leave your vehicle and head there. Once you reach that spot, lie down with your hands over your head. However, this is not the set of instructions to follow if the storm consists of heavy rain since the area can flood quickly. Always rely on your best judgment, as your gut instinct is the best one to follow in an emergency when you are equipped with prior knowledge.

USE COMMON SENSE

This is perhaps the most important part of dealing with severe weather. If you know of a storm coming, plan for activities that keep you out of the elements and in a safe and sheltered place. There are plenty of options no matter where you are traveling. If the warnings are too severe, simply pack up and leave if you still have time to put as much distance between you and the eye of the storm, if you will.

It is never worth the risk. So always do what keeps you safe. Severe weather can affect your plan, but it doesn't have to put you in the path of danger. When you are prepared and know how to react in severe weather, you'll stay safe while living on the road.

Thankfully, severe weather often doesn't last long, but there is always the chance of a natural disaster. Let's look at what you need to be prepared for in these extreme situations.

Preparing for a Natural Disaster

Natural disasters are always a threat and seem to be becoming more commonplace. RVs aren't as sturdy as traditional buildings and being in one during a natural disaster can be dangerous. Thankfully, there is plenty you can do to prepare for a natural disaster.

Avoiding a Natural Disaster

The first thing you need to do is avoid a natural disaster by avoiding bad weather when possible. This means avoiding areas where disaster is likely to strike and getting out of an area when bad weather is on the horizon. So, not visiting places known for having seasonal tornado season, or perhaps known for hurricane warnings in the past is the general rule of thumb to follow.

Being Prepared for Emergencies

There is always the chance that you won't be able to avoid a natural disaster at some point. So, a few suggestions to take into consideration:

- Have a reliable, thorough insurance plan.

- Keep your first-aid kit equipped with all the necessary items.

- Have an emergency go-bag on hand containing your first-aid kit, water, non-perishable food, a lighter or matches, your important documents, a can opener, and flashlights with their batteries.

- Keep a close eye on the weather through a great weather app.

RV Insurance

We've already discussed this in depth at a previous chapter, so I'm not going to tell you about it again. As a simple review: having good coverage isn't that difficult and is worth its price tag, particularly if you have valuables in your RV. Knowing the level of coverage you need before you shop for insurance is important; with good insurance coverage, you won't have to worry about your RV in an emergency and can instead focus on your family.

First-Aid Kit

A first-aid kit should always be on your list of preparation items. It is actually one of the most important pieces of equipment in your RV. This kit will help in a natural disaster as well as numerous other situations that can occur when you are exploring the great outdoors. The best first-aid kit should include the following:

☐ Various sized adhesive bandages

☐ Butterfly bandages

☐ Gauze

☐ Antiseptic creams and ointments

☐ Hydrogen peroxide

☐ Isopropyl alcohol

☐ Sterile wipes

☐ Rinse solutions

☐ Pain medication

☐ Hydrocortisone cream

☐ Tweezers

☐ Scissors

- [ ] Safety pins

- [ ] Knife

- [ ] Sunburn relief spray or cream

- [ ] Anti-diarrhea medicine

- [ ] Antihistamines

- [ ] Eye drops

- [ ] Moleskin

- [ ] Hand sanitizer

- [ ] Duct tape

- [ ] Super Glue

- [ ] Aloe vera

- [ ] Thread (both medical degree thread and sewing thread)

- [ ] Sunscreen

- [ ] Prescription medications if you have them

It is easy to put together a kit yourself, or you can purchase a premade kit. Just make sure you replace any items you use and ensure you inspect it regularly for expired items.

Since storms and natural disasters aren't something you might see every single day during your retirement in an RV, we covered a few precautions for the slight possibility that you might encounter them. But a far more present and problematic threat is that of a fire. As you may remember, RVs are known for being extremely flammable, which is why we will talk about fire safety in this incoming section.

RV FIRE SAFETY

The first thing you want to do is learn about the usual causes of fire in an RV, so you know what to prevent. Then you can focus on reducing your risks of an actual incident. As an RV owner, it is important to understand a fire can happen any time in a matter of seconds with a single careless circumstance and is one of the leading causes of death in this kind of vehicle.

The average RV is about 400 square feet and contains various flammable materials. In fact, the statistics show that it takes just 20 to 30 seconds for a fire to spread into a conflagration that people need to escape. Fire is very destructive and can start anywhere, so you need to know what to do should a fire start in your RV.

6 COMMON CAUSES OF RV FIRES

Every year, over 6,000 fires occur in RVs. The causes go as follows:

Propane Leaks. Propane is used to operate RV refrigerators, furnaces, ovens and stovetops. Propane is also highly flammable and doesn't take much to catch on fire. Fires typically happen from leaks in appliance or gas lines. Checking these lines regularly will help you to address problems before they become a major hazard. There are two precautions you need to take:

1. Brush gas lines with soapy water, and if you notice bubbles, this means you have a leak. Immediately close off the lines and seek immediate repairs.

2. If you smell propane, check that the pilot lights are lit and check everything to ensure all of it is properly turned off. If one of these is the source, then air out your RV and turn on your pilot light. On the other hand, if neither of these is an issue, open the windows and door before leaving the

coach and turning off the gas at the canister. Seek repairs as soon as possible.

It is a good idea to always keep updated gas leak detectors on your RV. If the gas leak is bad enough, the detector will give off a loud warning signal. If a fire starts, your smoke detector will sound as well. If you hear either of these alarms, it is best to evacuate the RV.

Leaking Fuel and Fluids Lines in Engines. Diesel RVs are more likely to leak fuel and fluids. Therefore they are more likely to catch fire. To protect against this problem, you should do the following:

- Check the engine compartment regularly.

- Have the engine professionally cleaned often.

- Have a fire suppression system installed in the engine compartment.

Wheels, Tires, and Brakes. Wheel bearings can dry up over time, and the resulting friction can cause fires. Lubricating the wheel bearings regularly will reduce the chance of this issue. Unmaintained tires can cause a blowout leading to an accident or flying debris that can start a fire. To lower the odds of that happening, make sure your tires aren't too old and check the air pressure regularly. Also, ascertain that the tires are all the same size and brand as part of the steps to protect the integrity of your tires.

Lastly, if you don't release your brakes when you drive your RV, the overheated rubber can catch fire. You'll likely smell the hot rubber in time to correct the issue, but if not, you'll need to take immediate action. It is recommended to bring a fire extinguisher on your travels.

Faulty Wiring. The various appliances in an RV take a lot of electrical wires to operate. As wires age, they become brittle and are prone to cracking. If this happens, they become prone to starting a fire. Again, you'll likely smell the wire burning before it actually catches fire, so inspecting the wires and fixing the problem before it becomes an issue is the best.

Otherwise, turn off the electricity if you smell a burning wire and investigate the problem to find the source and make repairs. To know if something is burning: it typically smells like burning plastic or a very pungent odor that is very hard to miss.

Cooking. Most people use their stovetops and ovens for RV cooking, but propane can catch fire easily since it is used exactly for controlled fires in these appliances. A spill or accidental placement of a potholder is all it takes to start a fire. You can make things safer by cooking with other methods aside from the stovetop and oven or to be extra careful not to miss anything as you cook. Remember, the fire extinguisher is your friend.

Highway Accidents. Accidents can result in fires if they are serious enough, and are often caused by four things:

1. Lack of driving skills

2. Influenced drivers

3. Poor road conditions

4. Bad weather

You can prevent the above by improving your driving skills, traveling over better roads, avoiding weather problems if possible, and being aware of other drivers around you. However, things can still happen, and you can still find yourself in trouble; in these situations, you need to know how to respond in a fire. Let's review the following ten tips.

10 TIPS TO PREVENT FIRE HAZARD

#1 - Know Where Trouble Starts. No matter what type of RV you own, you need to know the problem areas where fires start. For most RVs, the refrigerator and engine are the two main culprits. Electrical shorts are also a common problem, as well as kitchen fires from flammables such as curtains, towels, paper plates, and grease.

#2 - Have Fire Extinguishers. There are different types of fire extinguishers that can help fight fires in RVs. First is a dry chemical extinguisher that is a popular option for those living in an RV. It uses pressurized nitrogen to spray a fine powder over the fire. It is typically used on electrical fires and kitchen fires. However, the chemicals in these are toxic.

Another option is a CO2 or carbon dioxide extinguisher which works for various types of fires. They work by suffocating the fire through a high-pressure frost or dry ice. No matter which one you choose you should check them every six months and service them if you notice any pressure leaks.

#3 - Install an Automatic Extinguisher. You can also choose to install an automatic extinguisher to help you in an RV fire. These units are typically installed in the basement or storage area of an RV. This can provide you an extra level of safety in an RV fire.

#4 - Have an Exit Plan. You should always have two exit strategies in the event of an RV fire. Look at your windows and decide which ones are easy to open and which ones are safety windows. Once you get out of the RV what is the next step in the plan? Do you have a meeting place? Do you know how you will get your animals out? Practice your exit strategies and make sure you know what to do. If you have visitors over make sure they know the exit strategy as well.

#5 - Know How to Turn Things Off. Everyone who lives in your RV should know how to unhook electricity and close propane valves. They should also know where fire extinguishers are kept and how to use them. Ideally, there should be fire extinguishers in the bedroom, kitchen, and engine compartment. You may also want to have a fire extinguisher prepared and accessible outside the trailer while parked.

#6 - Know Your Location. When you get to a new place, make sure you get to know your location. Are there neighbors who can help in an emergency? Is there access to a phone? Are you parked around anything flammable? Doing this can help you stay safe and aware of your surroundings.

#7 - Install CO Detectors and Fire Alarms. CO (carbon dioxide) detectors and fire alarms save lives as long as you update them regularly. RVs can emit a range of unsafe gases, and a CO detector can help you avoid accidents.

#8 - Know How to Unhook Quickly. Whether you are towing a vehicle behind your RV or you are towing your RV trailer; you should know how to unhook your vehicle quickly in an emergency. Practice doing this and time yourself. The faster you can unhook, the better prepared you'll be in an emergency.

#9 - Certify the Propane System. Propane is primarily used to cook food and keep the refrigerator cold. Propane is easy to use, but it is also one of the deadliest things in an RV. Before moving your RV, make sure the propane tanks are shut off and always check your flue. Lastly, always have your propane system inspected and certified each year.

#10 - Properly Store Combustibles. Spontaneous combustion can happen with soiled rags, damp charcoal, batteries, and kitchen items. Flammable items should be kept in containers with lids and keep them away from the stove at all times.

By following these tips, you'll be prepared and know what to do in a variety of emergencies. This will make it safe for you to live on the road in your RV. Now the last thing to discuss is what you need to know to travel with your pets.

Anyone who has ever had pets knows that having them in a normal house comes with all sorts of situations varying in levels of difficulty, but traveling with temperamental pets can present a whole new set of challenges. Having your pets with you while living in an RV can be both the best and worst thing in your retirement since you are not only changing your way of living, but your pet's as well.

5 MUST DO'S

You have to think about that fact and prepare for your pet's safety, all while acclimating them to life on the road, which may not be a quick and simple process or one full of misery and eventual success depending on your pet. Let's look at five ways to prepare to keep your pet safe while on the road; then we'll look at how you can acclimate your pet to RV living.

#1 - SAFETY WHILE DRIVING

It may feel natural to let your pet roam free in the RV while you're driving between destinations, but this is actually quite dangerous. Even if you drive safe and follow all the rules of the road, there are plenty of unsafe drivers on the road.

If you were to get into an accident and your pet wasn't confined they could be severely injured. Plus, wandering pets could visit you on the driver's seat and cause a distraction. So make sure your pet is safely secured in a crate or seatbelt when the vehicle is moving.

#2 - KEEP A SUPPLY OF THE ESSENTIALS

If you are living with pets in an RV, don't forget to stay stocked up on their essentials. In addition to food and water, this also means leashes, waste bags, litter, toys, grooming supplies, and anything else your pet may need on a regular basis.

#3 - HAVE AN UPDATED ID

No matter how safe and secure you think your pet is, there is still a risk of them getting away from you. In this case, it is important that they have a microchip and have an updated form of ID on them. If you have them microchipped, make sure you keep the information up to date.

#4 - KEEP INFORMATION RECORDS

Just as you would with your important records, you want to keep all your pet's important records on hand as well. This means the following:

☐ Vaccination Records

☐ Proof of Ownership

☐ Photographs

In addition to these three things, you should also make sure you keep any medications your pet needs on hand as well. Add a second first-aid kit to your list of items to pack, since this one will be specifically for your pet.

#5 - DON'T SKIP THE EXERCISE

No matter what type of pet you are traveling with, driving and living in a small space can become boring. So make sure your pets get plenty of time to roam around once you are parked and find specific parks that allow pets so you can all enjoy the surrounding area.

Once you have everything you need for traveling with your pet, the next thing you need to do is make sure you acclimate them to living in an RV and life on the road.

5 STEPS TO ACCLIMATE YOUR PET TO RV LIFE

Pets can be a great companion for someone living on the road. As long as you implement the safety features above there is no reason they can't come along. However, it may be challenging for your pet to get used to the RV. To make it easier, consider the following five tips.

#1 - UNDERSTAND YOUR PET'S PERSONALITY

The RV can be as comfortable as a house, and for humans, it can be easy to make the switch. Yet, there still are people who enter a phase of shock at the idea of not living in one fixed place. The transition comes with its challenges for us, let alone for our pets like our dogs and cats who can't switch over to a new environment as easily as we can.

If your pet has never traveled before, the RV is going to be a new and potentially scary place for them. There are a few things you need to consider before taking your pet on the road.

How Does Your Pet Do in Different Environments?

Are your pets the type that are happy no matter where they go? Do they do well traveling between your home and the veterinary office or boarding kennel? Are your pets curious when you open the front door or do they cower in fear? Do they require any type of sedation for a minor car ride?

While pets with this behavior can learn to acclimate in time, you will need to be patient and gradual in your introduction to the RV lifestyle.

Acquaint Your Pet to the RV

Start the process by placing some of your pet's belongings in the RV and then bringing them inside to let them sniff around and get their scent on things. If your dog is crate trained, bring the crate inside and encourage them to go inside. If your pet shows signs of being anxious, sit with them for a while and calm them down before letting them explore further.

You can also associate the RV with good things by feeding them treats or having a small playful interaction each time. Return to your home and gradually increase the length of time you spend in the RV until your pet is more comfortable with their environment. This may take a few tries, or it can take a month, it depends on the individual pet.

Prepare them for Noise

Once your pet is acclimated to being inside the RV, the next thing you need to do is introduce the concept of noise and motion. If possible, try to have one person stay with the pet while the other drives; but don't start driving down the road just yet. Bring your pet into the RV and allow them to settle first. Then turn on the engine. Allow the engine to run for a few minutes so you can see how your pet reacts.

Some pets are fine with this, but others will be nervous right away. If they respond well, offer them treats then repeat the process a few times throughout the week. If they freak out, stop the engine immediately and stay with the pet until they calm down and know the quiet is returning.

Introduce the Concept of Motion

Now you want to actually get on the road. Start with the previous two steps. Once the pet is calm, take a short drive around the block. Make sure your pet is in a safe and secure place before you move.

As you drive, ignore any anxious behavior and reward any calm and quiet behavior with praise and treats. Gradually increase the length of your trips until your pet is comfortable with them.

#2 - HAVE A PET-FRIENDLY ENVIRONMENT

Animals are naturally curious and often get into trouble while at home. The risk is even greater when they are placed in a new environment such as an RV. The compact nature of an RV makes it easier for your pets to get into everything. There are a few things you can do to reduce these risks.

Crate Train

A crate gives your pet a comfortable and den-like environment, or a home-like a place for them. A crate allows your pet to calm down and relax during the ride. Crate training is important for ongoing success, and it is never too late to train them on this. Find a dry, cozy, quiet place in the RV and cover it with one of your old shirts, so it is scented like you.

There are also certain calming pet-oriented essential oils that you can sprinkle on their den with so they feel more relaxed. Careful with these oils, though, as they vary from pet species and too much of them could be harmful to your pet's health. Read the instructions and ask your vet about one particular brand before actually using it.

Avoid Food Temptation

RV refrigerators offer plenty of tempting food treats for pets. Make sure you put away any food that your pets can get into if you aren't going to be inside the vehicle for a few minutes.

Have a Cat House

If you have cats, you may want to consider have a cat house observation deck installed in the basement area. This allows your pet to travel between the safety of the basement and the interior of the RV as much as they please. You can also screen in the basement areas so they can have fresh air without having to venture into the outdoors.

Finding a Bathroom Spot for Your Cat

If you have an indoor cat that is used to a litter box you can still find room for one in your RV. Technically-speaking, litter boxes do not have a natural predisposition to stink. They only need proper maintenance, as they would in a house or anywhere else. This maintenance procedure consists of the following:

- Clean the litter box twice a day (or every time your cat drops solid waste as not to let the odor linger).

- Choose cat litter that clumps quickly and retains bad odors. Whether it is scented or unscented, it depends on you and your cat's preferences, but if you choose a scented brand make sure it is more on the clean, crisp detergent-smell spectrum than the overly sweet floral one.

- Once every two weeks, you must empty the litter box entirely and dispose of the sand, followed by a deep scrub to thoroughly clean the empty box with a brush, water, and pet-friendly products. Allow the box to dry, then fill it back up with fresh, clean sand.

These procedures will ensure you have a pleasant-smelling RV that is comfortable for you and for your pets.

Harnesses, Leashes, and Pet Tags

Whether you have a dog or cat, you should use a harness and leash to ensure their safety when outdoors. And they should always have pet tags to identify them in case they get away from you.

#3 - MONITOR YOUR PETS HEALTH

When living in an RV, your pet's health should be one of your top priorities and also goes a long way to acclimate them to life on the road. Depending on where you travel, there can be new viruses, diseases, and illnesses. Make the acclimation process easier for your pet by doing the following.

Prepare for Emergencies

Some pets get so anxious they have gastrointestinal issues. This can cause a decrease in appetite along with diarrhea and vomiting in some cases. You should address these potential issues before you head out on the road for a long trip so you can have medications ready if needed.

#4 - BE CONSISTENT

Pets do best with consistency and constantly traveling can be difficult to keep a schedule, but there are some things you can do to help provide consistency for your pet while living in an RV.

Have a Routine for Arrival

When you first get to a site, set up the same way each time. This will not only make your setup easier, but it will also give your pet a sense of routine. After set up, spend some time with your pet, so they get attention and appreciation. When breaking down your site, allow your pets to watch.

Consistent Activities

Dogs, in particular, like to have regular times for walks, meals, and play; but cats can enjoy this consistency as well in their eating and play-time schedule as well as your sleeping schedule, so they know when to start winding down. While it can be difficult to do this on the road, your pet will acclimate a lot easier if you are consistent in their day to day activities.

#5 - BE RESPONSIBLE

Lastly, when you travel with your pet, be a responsible pet owner. Be courteous to your neighbors and keep your pet as controlled as possible. Don't leave your pet alone for long periods of time, as that would be too stressful for them.

As a whole just remember your pet does not understand what is happening as well as you do. All they know is one day they were in their home; then everything started disappearing until they found themselves in a strange, noisy contraption and miles of road ahead.

Take your time in acclimating them before actually starting your trip, and put their needs first at all times. These furry critters are a part of your family, and they ought to be treated with as much love, patience, and understanding as you can manage, so they are healthy and happy in a situation they did not pick for themselves.

With all of that said, it's time to cover exactly, what you need to do when you find a place you want to set up for a few days, weeks, or even months.

CHOOSING PLACES TO STAY

When you live in an RV, you are going to travel a lot, but you are also going to settle down from time to time. Whether you stay in a place for days, weeks or months there are several options available. Let's consider the types of places you can stay at and how to set up your site when you arrive.

TYPES OF PLACES TO STAY

Living from an RV means you are going to need a place to stay at some point. The amount of time you plan to spend there and the type of lifestyle you are looking for will have an impact on where you choose to stay. Let's look at the options available to you to help you understand what is available.

When you are traveling around by RV, you are likely going to plan your destinations and stay in an area a while to see all the sights. However, there will also be times when you just need a place to park for the night so you can rest and get back on the road the next day. If this is the case, there are six places where you can park for a night for free.

#1 - Truck Stops. You can find these spread throughout the country and are often located near major highways so you can easily stop in for an overnight rest before getting back on the road. You can also get fuel, food, and other basic supplies as needed. A few truck stops will also have an area where you can dump your waste tanks.

#2 - Retail Chain Stores. Walmart is well-known among RV travelers as a convenient place to spend the night. Occasionally there may be local ordinances, and in those cases, there are signs that show no overnight parking is allowed. Walmart stores are available in most cities and also function as a place to restock supplies if needed. There are also other large chain stores that will most likely allow you to stay overnight in their lot if you just go inside and speak with the store manager first.

#3 - Restaurants. A lot of restaurants located near major roadways have extra parking for larger rigs and may allow you to spend the night. Most of these places will also have free internet access so you can grab some food and check your emails before you go to sleep for the night.

#4 - RV Parts and Service Stores. There are plenty of national chains such as Camping World that not only offer the supplies and parts you need for your RV but also offer overnight parking in their lots. So if you need to make repairs, you can do it while also getting some rest before heading back out on the road.

#5 - Casinos. While casinos aren't as prevalent, most do have parking set aside for RVs. As long as you head inside for a little gambling or to grab a bite in the actual premises, they typically don't care how long you stay in the parking lot.

#6 - Small Towns. Most small towns are open to RV travelers. You'll find local city parks or other RV facilities that allow you to stay free for a night.

These are excellent places if you just need to spend the night and rest before going for another long drive. However, once you get where you are going, and you want to stay a while, there are different options to consider. Let's look at what these could be.

RV RESORTS

A place that is labeled as an RV resort is likely to have extra features you won't normally get at other RV parks. This can sometimes include things like cable TV, swimming pools, tennis courts, and sometimes even a golf course. These places tend to be more selective about who they allow to stay, and you may need to make reservations in advance.

RV Parks

These options tend to be a little more park-like than an RV resort and have less high-end amenities. They still offer spacious and well kept up sites for your RVs. Most come with full hookup sites, but not all. Another pro is that they are considerably cheaper than an RV resort and will be equipped with most of what you need instead of paying extra for overly luxurious accommodations.

Campgrounds

There is camping available at state and national campgrounds. Many of these are only a step up from primitive camping with limited hookups. Electricity tends to be the most common hookup, with water and sewer hookups being less likely.

Most campgrounds have dump facilities on site, however. Because some camping sites may not be large or leveled enough to accommodate all RVs, it is best not to assume you will immediately find a spot here. On the bright side, if they cannot accommodate you, someone will most likely tell you where to go to find such a place.

BOONDOCKING

Boondocking is also known as dry camping. This requires rugged and off-grid camping without any form of amenities. Only those with serious knowledge and ability to camp off the grid should attempt this form of RV living.

10 THINGS TO CONSIDER BEFORE CHOOSING AN RV PARK

Not all RV parks are the same, contrary to popular belief. Typically, the one you choose to stay at depends greatly on your personal preferences and your RV requirements for maintenance and upkeep. Let's look at the steps you need to take to help you choose an RV park when you are ready to head to your next place.

Research

Before you start the next stage of your adventure, determine where you want to stop. Then look up RV parks in the general area. Look up reviews of the parks and save the names of the ones that have better reviews. Look up details such as amenities, cost, and size of RVs allowed. This will go a long way to narrowing down your options.

Location

Most RV parks are located along the outskirts of busy areas, but some nice parks tend to be further out in the suburbs of the town. If you don't plan to leave your RV often, being far away from a city center doesn't tend to be that big of a deal. However, if there is something you want to explore, pick an RV park that is close to that area of interest.

Budget

While staying at an RV park is far cheaper than staying in a hotel, there is quite a variation in price between RV parks. So plan on how much you have to spend for the length of time you want to stay and choose an RV park that fits within your budget.

Modern or Rustic Park

What is your preference for style? Do you like to be close to nature? Or do you prefer to have all of the modern conveniences? Knowing this will help you choose which RV park you want to stay at. There are some parks that blend both scenarios into a single location, but your personal preference might have you prefer one over another.

Hookups

Perhaps one of the biggest appeals to staying in an RV park over camping is the fact that you have hookups for electricity, water, and sewer. Not all parks have the same hookups available so you should research what is available and if there is any additional charge for them.

Internet

Internet availability at an RV park may or may not be a big issue for you. If you want to stay connected to family and friends but don't have a decent connection through your cell phone or another plan, you may want to consider an RV park that offers a stable internet connection as its amenities.

Family-Friendly

This may be less of a concern if you are retired and traveling, but if you plan to have family visiting or if you are taking a break and have the grandkids with you then you should look for a park that is family-friendly. This way you know there are activities to keep everyone busy. Although if you want peace and quiet, you may want to avoid the family-friendly parks as there will be children playing near you unless that is not something that would interrupt your inner peace.

Facilities

While most RVs are self-contained, it is still nice to have an RV park with clean and well-appointed restrooms. This is especially true if you plan to stay in the area for a longer period of time. Consider the size of the bathrooms, their overall cleanness, and whether or not hot showers are included in the cost of the stay.

Social Connections

Some RV parks offer a roster of planned activities so that you can enjoy your time with the other guests. For some, this is an attraction because you can make new friends and exercise the social part of your personality. For others, this is a turn-off since they prefer the solitude and quiet of being outdoors.

Take a Look

Lastly, you may just need to pull into the park and ask to take a look around before actually deciding to pay the fee in order to stay. This will give you a general feel for the area and the park itself. During your look-around it is recommended you ask the following questions to make sure it is everything you want and need:

- What does a standard site cost and what amenities does it offer?

- Are the sites pull-through or back-in?

- What size of RVs can the sites accommodate?

- Are pets allowed? (If this applies to you)

- What extra fees are there aside from the daily advertised rates?

- How long are you allowed to stay and can you extend your time?

- Are there shady sites or are they all in the sun?

- What is the noise level?

- What amenities are there and what times are they available?

- Are there any organized activities?

After this, you should have a good idea of where you want to stay. Once you are pulled into your site and parked, it's time to get set up. Let's take a look at this process next.

LEVELING AND STABILIZING YOUR RV

If your RV comes with electric or hydraulic levelers, the process of stabilizing and leveling your RV is a lot easier. On the other hand, if you need to manually level and stabilize your RV, it isn't too difficult with a simple process. The most important thing to remember before we start is that you always want at least one tire on the ground. You may not even need to do this process if you stay at an RV park where the parking pad is pre-leveled.

Once you've pulled into your site, turn off the engine and set the parking brake. Make sure you are about two or three feet from where you want to stay parked.

Get out of your RV and examine the ground. Determine how many blocks you think you need and which side of the RV needs to be lifted. Take the time to really assess the situation since it can take a few tries to get it right.

Place your leveling blocks up against the tires that you want to raise. If you are stacking them, put them together like stepping Legos. Remember that you want to drive up them like a ramp.

Return to your RV and start the engine then release the brake. Slowly accelerate up the blocks. When you reach the center of the blocks, stop. It is best to have someone guide you through the process to make it easier.

Go outside once more to evaluate the situation. Is the RV level? Does something need to be raised or lowered? If so, you may need to back up and try again.

After you are settled, you may set your parking brake and turn off the engine.

By this point, you can go about setting up your campsite. Let's see how you can set up a nice home at your campsite since you might be there a while.

SETTING UP A CAMPSITE

The first step after getting pulled into your site and leveled is to set up your RV:

1. Disconnect your tow vehicle.

2. Set down the stabilizer jacks.

3. Disconnect the battery on your chassis.

4. Use a voltmeter to test the voltage of the electricity.

5. Plug the RV into the receptacle that matches the amperage requirements.

6. Ensure electricity is working.

7. Turn on your refrigerator.

8. Hook up the water regulator to the water supply.

9. Ensure water is flowing into your RV.

10. Wear protective equipment and attach the sewer hose to the drain outlet.

11. Turn on the supply of propane.

12. Hook up your cable if this is provided by the campground.

13. Set up your outdoor campsite.

MAINTAINING AND REPAIRING YOUR RV

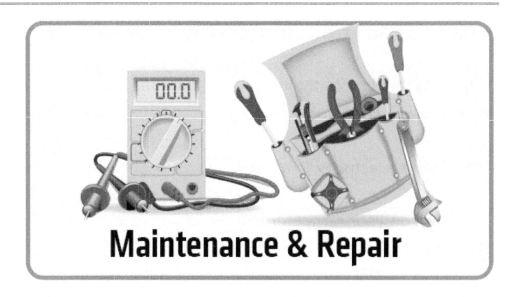

Maintenance & Repair

Maintaining and repairing your RV can be an expensive process, but with the right tools and the right guidance, you can keep your RV in great shape so you can have a great place to live in for a time. Let's look at some of the basic maintenance and repair you can do yourself to save money on hiring someone to fix it for you.

MUST-HAVE TOOLS

Having specific items in your toolbox will pull you out of otherwise gnarly situations more often than you might expect, and will help you deal with basic repairs as well as some emergencies. At a minimum you should carry the following five items:

1. Small Tools

2. Air Compressor

3. Tire Gauge

4. Wheel Chocks

5. Rear Camera Monitoring System

LIST OF SMALL TOOLS YOU MUST HAVE

There are some basic small tools that you should always carry in your RV. Most of these items will fit in a portable tool kit so it shouldn't take up too much space in your limited room.

☐ Pliers

☐ Blade Fuses

☐ Protective gloves

☐ Tire-changing equipment

☐ Vise-grips

☐ Wrenches

☐ Wire brush

☐ Box cutter

- ☐ Razor blades

- ☐ Pry bar

- ☐ Hammer

- ☐ Small saw

- ☐ Tube of silicone

- ☐ Hose clamps

- ☐ Screwdrivers

- ☐ Nails, screws, nuts, bolts

- ☐ Adjustable wrench

- ☐ Bungee cords

- ☐ Small shovel

- ☐ Zip ties

- ☐ Rope

- ☐ Electrical tape

- ☐ Duct tape

- ☐ Tape measure

☐ Voltage meter

☐ Water pressure gauge

☐ Extra hoses

AIR COMPRESSOR

One of the most important things an RV owner can know how to maintain and use is tires. This includes knowing how and when to inflate them without causing damage. It is a good idea to have an air compressor on your RV since gas station air compressors don't put enough air out to properly inflate RV tires.

Also, public air pumps often have water in them, which can ruin your vehicle in general. With a personal air compressor, you can care for your own tires as well as air up other items such as beds, rafts, and other things that require inflation. You ideally want a 150-pound compressor to adequately inflate your RV tires.

TIRE GAUGE

This is another important item to have to maintain and care for your tires. The same one you use for cars will work for an RV. Make sure you test it regularly in order to make sure it is working accurately. If you aren't comfortable reading a tire gauge, you can install a wireless system.

When on the road, check your tire pressure several times a day. If your tires aren't equally inflated, you have a greater chance of a blowout, leading to a potential accident.

WHEEL CHOCKS

This is perhaps the cheapest and most helpful piece of equipment you'll keep on your RV. They are cheap, lightweight, and come in a range of sizes. Properly used, they can prevent damage to your RV from unstable parking conditions. It is best to have a backup set on hand in case one breaks. You should never park your RV without wheel chocks.

REAR CAMERA MONITORING SYSTEM

You should consider having a rear camera monitoring system installed. Having something like that can help ensure your tow vehicle is securely connected when traveling, and it can make it easier to back into your campsite. Just make sure the screen is big enough for you to see comfortably.

Packing these basics is a must for any RV toolbox. You'll be surprised how often you use these items. Although this isn't a one-size-fits-all sort of list; perhaps you will find there is another tool you need or one that isn't needed in your case. Feel free to customize as needed. However, a proper toolkit is only effective if you combine it with a regular maintenance schedule.

BEFORE YOU HIT THE ROAD
RV Maintenance Checklist

Appliances

☒ Refrigerator
☒ Inspect door seals
☒ Inspect burner flame
☒ Clean thermocouple tip
☒ Clean area behind refrigerator
☒ Furnace
☒ Check blower
☒ Check combustion chamber
☒ Check control compartment
☒ Inspect gas line
☒ Air conditioning unit
☒ Clean air filters
☒ Clean condensing unit
☒ Check voltage
☒ Hot water heater
☒ Flush every 6 months
☒ Clean burner tube
☒ Inspect sacrificial electrode
☒ Stove
☒ Make sure it produces blue flames
☒ Clear vents of animal nests and debris

Walkaround

☒ Inspect roof/body for cracks
☒ Check all lights and turn signals
☒ Check gas levels in propane tanks
☒ Charged fire extinguisher
☒ Test smoke detectors
☒ Test carbon monoxide detectors

General Maintenance

Check:
☒ Engine oil
☒ Transmission oil
☒ Tire pressure
☒ Tire wear
☒ Battery
☒ Brake fluid
☒ Power steering fluid
☒ Engine belts
☒ Engine coolant
☒ Windshield washer fluid

Plumbing

☒ Check that water pump flows well
☒ Flush waste tanks
☒ Inspect valves and water pump for leaks
☒ Inspect connection dump hose and fittings
☒ Sanitize water system

Having a regular maintenance schedule is important to the safe functioning of your RV. There are a few things you need to do daily to make sure your engine is running well and safe. Then there are quarterly maintenance checks that look into the other main parts of your RV.

FOUR DAILY ENGINE CHECK ITEMS

The RV engine is a complicated piece of equipment, but with four daily preventative checks, you can avoid some of the most common causes of breakdown. A daily engine check should only take about five minutes. It may not be necessary every day, but should definitely be done any time you are going to be driving for longer than an hour. Let's look at the four items you can cross off your checklist.

#1 - Engine Oil

The engine oil is what keeps the components of the engine lubricated. Having the right amount will prevent damage to the engine. Find the engine oil dipstick handle and pull it out, wipe it clean with a fresh rag and reinsert it all the way in before pulling out again. There will be two lines on the stick: "ADD" and "FULL."

The oil should be covering the stick between these two lines. If it is below the "ADD" line, then you want to add engine oil. If it is over the "FULL" line, then you'll want to drain some engine oil. Too much oil is just as damaging as too little since it can blow a head gasket.

#2 - Coolant

As you may have guessed by the name, the coolant helps to keep the engine cool while driving. Your temperature gauge will most likely give you a warning if there is a leak and you start to overheat. If this happens, you should stop your RV immediately. This is why you should check it before getting on the road.

The coolant reservoir is often a semi-opaque white tank near the radiator. Unscrew the cap and look inside to see where the level is at. Again, there will be two lines labeled "ADD" and "FULL." As with the engine oil, the coolant should be between these two lines. If the coolant is low, add more and check it again the next day to see if there is a leak that needs to be addressed.

#3 - Serpentine Belt

This drives most of the components of the engine like the radiator fan, the alternator, and the coolant pump. Problems tend to occur if the belt is old and brittle to the point where it cracks while driving. To check it simply locate it; it is a long thin piece of material that wraps around pulleys and the components of your engine.

Find a spot where you can grab it and gently pull the belt to check tension. It shouldn't be too tight or too loose, and there should be no visible cracks. If it is too loose or tight, it will need to be adjusted, and any cracks or brittle sensations mean it needs to be replaced.

#4 - Brake Fluid

This isn't exactly a part of the engine, but it is in the same compartment and should be checked. The brake fluid causes your brake pads to press against the calipers and therefore stops your vehicle. The correct amount of brake fluid is important to the operation of your brakes. Find the brake fluid reservoir; typically another small semi-opaque tank that visibly has liquid in it with a cap that says DOT 3 FLUID or BRAKE FLUID. On the outside of the tank there will be two lines labeled "minimum" and "maximum."

The fluid should be between these two lines. If the level is under the minimum line, then there may be a leak. The lower your brake fluid is at, the more it indicates a need to replace your brake pads.

These four simple checks will allow you to avoid unnecessary breakdowns and costly repairs. So take the five minutes to do these four things before heading out on the road.

QUARTERLY MAINTENANCE

There are many benefits to have a regular RV maintenance schedule. It will not only make your RV safer but also more comfortable to live in. It will increase the life of your RV and reduce the cost of repairs. Let's look at some quarterly maintenance steps.

Keep Records

Keep a log of all your maintenance activities, especially those related to the safety and integrity of the RV. Include the date and what checks were performed as well as any repairs or replacements that were performed. The logbook will provide proof of the things you've done and show you've taken good care of your RV.

Quarterly Maintenance Checklist

It is important to note that every RV is different. Check your owner's manual for specific recommended maintenance. Let's look into some of the basics that should be on your maintenance checklist.

Electrical System. Make sure you are connected to power before running a basic safety test on the electrical system. Start with checking the circuit breaker and each fuse to make sure they are connected and working. Then test each outlet, light, and appliance in the RV. If something isn't working, you probably have an electrical problem. If the stove or furnace has an electric starter, check those as well. Lastly, check the voltage on your battery to make sure it is properly charging.

Propane System. If an RV has a propane gas system, it also should have a propane leak detection system. The sensor is often located near the floor since propane gas is heavier than air and will therefore sink. Start your test by making sure the detector is powered. To check for leaks, open the main propane valve, close the doors and windows and wait for about two hours. If the alarm goes off, then you have a leak somewhere, and you should get it fixed right away. While two hours may sound like a long time, just think of it as the duration of a movie, or a few chapters from a fantastic book and the minutes will pass by in a flash.

Appliances. You should do a functional and visual inspection of all your major appliances. Turn on each burner on the stove, use the microwave, and look at the refrigerator temperature and anything else you need to check on appliances. At the same time, you should appropriately clean each appliance and listen for any unusual sounds. If there is anything out of the ordinary have it addressed right away.

Brakes. It is important that you learn how to do a visual inspection of your brakes. Start by researching the type of brakes you have on your RV, so you know what to look for when inspecting them. The most common thing you are searching for is worn brake pads. You may also want to do a live braking test to see if you feel any irregularities. If you have a trailer, you need to clean your brake connector with contact cleaner. This can also be the best time to check the breakaway switch and ensure it appears in good order.

Hinges and Locks. Every 90 days you should apply lubricant to the hinges and locks on your RV. Something like WD-40 is fine. You won't need much and make sure you wipe away any excess with a paper towel to avoid streaks and stains. Use a dry graphite lubricant for locks.

Lug Nuts. Research the proper torque rating for the lug nuts on the wheels of your RV and make a note on your checklist. Use a mechanical or hydraulic torsion wrench to make sure you have the right torque on each lug nut. This is best done by lifting the wheel off the ground, but you can make initial adjustments by moving the vehicle, so it rotates the tire 180 degrees then making the next adjustment.

Power Wash. You should give your RV a good exterior wash at least once every three months. This is also a good time to apply wax or other treatments as recommended by the manufacturer. Other recommended activities involve cleaning the undercarriage, wheels, and roof as best as you can to avoid rust and damage. Dirt left in these places can also lead to corrosion so scrub these as much as you can to keep it squeaky clean and pristine.

Mileage Check. If you don't travel a lot, but spend most of your time parked at a site, a quarterly mileage check is fine. Most RVs will have an engine and brake recommendation based on mileage. To get the most out of your RV, follow these recommendations as closely as possible and make an appointment for service when the mileage is close.

Tires. Tires should be checked before you head out on the road. Tires with 50 percent or less tread wear should be changed. Ascertain your tire pressure is correct to the recommendations from the manufacturer.

This is just what you need to check for maintenance purposes. What about the need for repairs? If something goes wrong, would you know what to do? We are going to look at some specific maintenance and repairs that you can do on your own to save some money.

RV HOLDING TANKS AND HOSES

We've already discussed a lot about dumping and cleaning your gray and black tanks, but another issue that comes up often for RV owners is the protection and storage of the hoses used for all three RV tanks. It is important that you know the functions of each hose and use common sense when cleaning, storing, and protecting them.

WATER HOSES

First, you don't want to use the standard green water hose for your drinkable water since it will cause any liquid that passes through it to have a rubbery taste. You should use a white hose since they are designed to carry fresh water to your RV. Those new to RVing often think you simply need to coil the hoses and put them on the basement floor, BUT doing this will cause four issues:

1. Water can leak onto the floor.

2. Dirt, debris, and bugs can get into the hose.

3. Retrieving the hose can be difficult.

4. Handling the hose can become a dirty job.

Instead, you want a clean and secure environment for storing your equipment. Use the following steps to do so:

1. Rinse dirt off the hose's exterior before storing it.

2. Drain as much water as possible.

3. Coil the hose tightly.

4. Tie a piece of rope around the coiled hose.

5. Place a plastic bag over each end and secure them with rubber bands.

6. Place the hose in a painter's bucket and put a lid on it.

When you do these six steps, you will be keeping your white hose clean and sanitary for each use.

GRAY AND BLACK WATER HOSES

The gray tank holds used, dirty water and the black tank holds waste. When you dump either of these tanks, the material will exit through the same hose known as the sewer hose. There are two handles you pull on your RV to release the contents, and you pull one at a time. Whenever you are staying in your RV you should keep the sewer tank closed and the gray tank open.

When it is time to dump the tanks, you close the gray tank and run some clean soapy water into it. Then you pull the handle to empty the black tank and backwash it as we already described.

After you are finished, wash the interior of the hose by opening the gray tank and allowing the soapy water to empty through the sewer hose. Then you can close both tanks and unhook the sewer hose for proper storage.

As with your water hose, you want to keep sewer hoses clean and free of debris because they can build up bad odors and dangerous bacteria. We already discussed how to wash the sewer hose, but now we need to discuss storage.

Most RVs have a built-in bumper or another area where you can securely store this hose. You should always carry a spare to connect to your main one in case you need to reach a dump outlet. Since the built-in storage area only fits one hose, you'll need to find another way to store the second.

You can purchase a heavy plastic hose carrier that you can attach to the underside of your RV. You can also make your own holder from a PVC pipe.

Now that we know how to store our hoses, the only tank maintenance we haven't discussed is that of the freshwater tank. Here goes nothing, right?

FRESH WATER TANK MAINTENANCE

Of the three tanks in an RV, the one that requires the least maintenance and upkeep is the freshwater tank. This also means it is most likely to be ignored, depending on the type of person you are. While there isn't much that goes into cleaning and sanitizing this tank, it still needs to be done regularly. Doing so will help reduce your chances of getting ill or finding a bug in your tea. To clean and sanitize your tank use the following steps:

1. Completely drain the tank.

2. Remove your water filter, discard it if there is tainted water.

3. Add ¼ cup bleach to one gallon of water and pour it all into the tank.

4. Fill to the top with clean water.

5. Open each faucet individually starting with the cold than the hot water. Wait until the chlorine smell comes out.

6. Turn off each faucet.

7. Run a cycle through the empty washing machine if you have one.

8. Allow the system to sit for four hours.

9. Drain the system.

10.   Flush with fresh water until the smell of chlorine is gone.

11.   If needed, install a new water filter.

MANAGING WATER DAMAGE AND MOISTURE

Water damage can be damaging to the structure of your RV. You need to regularly look for leaks and do what you can to reduce moisture inside the RV. When it comes to checking for leaks you want to look for the following:

- Rusted metal items.

- Damp carpets.

- Ceiling discoloration.

- Loose moldings.

- Rust stains on the windows and skylights.

- Spongy areas on the roof.

- Sidewall indentation.

- Bubbling or discoloration.

You can also head off water damage before it happens by reducing moisture levels in the RV. You can do this in six simple steps.

1. Keep the RV well-ventilated.

2. When cooking, open the window next to the area to let steam out and keep lids on pans when cooking.

3. When you shower, open the roof vent and window (if you have one) to let steam out.

4. If possible, leave a roof vent or window open when you sleep at night.

5. Wipe up excess moisture right away.

6. Don't create excess water or steam.

These are simple and easy ways to reduce water and moisture build up. Plus if you see any signs of water damage, you should have the RV inspected for leaks and repaired immediately before the damage gets worse.

ROOF MAINTENANCE AND CARE

You should regularly climb on top of your RV and inspect your roof. Knowing the type of material is important since it will tell you what type of damage to look for.

Along with the roof, in general, you should re-caulk seams at least once a year. If you notice any issues with the roof they must be repaired immediately as this can lead to structural damage within the RV.

BATTERY MAINTENANCE AND CARE

Just like the entire vehicle, the batteries require regular preventative maintenance. Use the following checklist when performing maintenance on your RV batteries.

- **Inspect Connections.** Check the batteries and the whole compartment with all visible wires. All the movement of an RV can easily cause connections to come loose.

- **Check for Damage.** Look for loose wires, frayed wires, cracked battery cases, spilled battery fluid or battery acid build-up on the terminals.

- **Battery Fluid Level.** Check all battery fluid levels before any road trip and refill any cells that are low with distilled water.

- **Ready for the Road.** Before you drive away, always make sure all battery connectors are tight and free from any oxidation residue.

- **Residual Current Leakage.** Even if you aren't using your batteries, low currents will leak and discharge your batteries over time.

- **Regular Inspections.** While you are staying at an RV park or campground, you should check your batteries every two to four weeks. Particularly the fluid levels.

- **Monthly Engine Start.** If you are camping an extended period, you should also start your RV at least once a month and run it for 30 minutes to keep the engine system lubricated and to recharge the chassis batteries.

As you already know, RV tires require extra maintenance and different type of care than regular car tires. Consider the following tips to help you properly maintain and care for your tires.

- If you are going to stay somewhere for a while, you should park on wood, concrete, or gravel rather than dirt.

- Use a tire gauge to regularly check your tire pressure, so all tires are equally inflated.

- Ensure the tires on your RV are rated properly to carry the weight of your RV.

- Wash your tires regularly to remove as much dirt and debris from the treads as possible.

- Never lift your RV on jacks to take the weight off your tires, this will damage the structure of your vehicle.

- Tires can overheat in hot weather so you should travel in cooler weather, or stop to give the tires time to cool down. Another option is to hose them down with cold water to avoid expansion and blowouts while driving.

A/C MAINTENANCE

You may not use your air conditioning all that often if you travel to temperate climates. However, you should still maintain and clean it regularly to help upkeep your RV and have it ready to go for when you do need to use it. There are four steps involved in cleaning the air conditioner:

1. Have your air conditioner is unplugged before you start to clean it.

2. Clean the filters. If you use your air conditioner often, clean the filter at least once a month. To clean, wash them gently with warm water and allow them to air dry. If you notice they are torn or damaged, buy new ones.

3. Clean the evaporator coils. Once you remove the filters, you'll be able to see these. Remove any dirt or debris with a soft bristle brush found on vacuums.

4. Clean the condenser coils. Climb onto the roof of our RV and detach the shroud from the air conditioner unit. Vacuum out the dust and spray the coils with a specific coil cleaner.

Here are five things you can do to increase the life of your air conditioner:

1. **Manage your thermostat settings.**

   When operating it at a moderate setting, it will perform better and last longer.

2. **Open the roof vent on occasion.**

   When you don't need to run the air conditioner, open up a roof vent and allow the moisture to evaporate. This can prevent damage to the air conditioner and reduce moisture buildup in the RV.

3. **Check the condenser twice a year.**

   Check this for clogs on a regular basis, and if the air conditioner still isn't cooling it will most likely need to be replaced.

4. Oil the fan.

This part of the air conditioner works hard, so you should keep it well-oiled.

5. Cover the unit in the offseason.

When you aren't using the air conditioner, keep it covered.

HOW TO SAVE MONEY AND LIVE AFFORDABLY IN AN RV

Most people choose to live in an RV because it saves money over living in a traditional house and it gives you greater freedom in retirement. To save money and live more affordably in your RV I have prepared the following tips that you always can use as an inspiration or as the foundation of a brainstorming session or plan more adapted to your individual lifestyle and preferences.

How to Save Money on Fuel

- Try to avoid driving into strong winds since it increases drag and causes you to burn more fuel.

- Keep your speed down since driving over 55 in a large vehicle like an RV can burn more fuel and lead to unsafe situations.

- Choose routes with the fewest stop lights, so you aren't stopping and accelerating often.

- Have the tires inflated to the right pressure.

- Don't weigh down your RV, since a heavier RV means worse mileage.

How to Save Money on Maintenance

- Have regular oil changes performed.

- Replace old or worn tires.

- Do as many small repairs on your own as you can.

- Do not stall in your repairs.

How to Save Money on Places to Stay

- Travel in the offseason when rates are lower.

- Try to stay for at least a week or more to get lower costs per night.

- Stay at state parks or other public campgrounds since you'll have limited hookups at a cheaper cost.

- Don't pay for amenities you won't use.

- Ask for lower rates if you are going to stay for a longer period of time.

- Offer word trade instead of payment for staying at RV parks.

- Consider boondocking or dry camping.

HOW TO SAVE MONEY ON FOOD

- Limit the number of times you eat at restaurants.

- Pack snacks to take with you in the day for lunch.

- Don't overbuy groceries.

- Buy dry products or non-perishables you eat regularly in bulk if possible.

- Use a crockpot to cook while you're gone for the day and freeze leftovers for the next day.

- If you are going to be spending a lot of time outdoors, consider getting National Park passes or other similar passes.

- Head to the visitors' center to get information on free or low-cost attractions in the area.

- Look for discount days for local attractions.

CONCLUSION

I've now spent a good deal of this book talking to you about the best way to do things and how to be the best when living from your RV. In conclusion, I want to switch and tell you the ten most common mistakes to avoid. I've made many of these, and I'm sure all of them have been made by first-time RVers. Hopefully, by telling you about them, you can avoid making the same mistakes.

Too Far, Too Fast. You are retired and living from your RV, so you don't need to rush. There is no need to cram things into a small vacation window. Remember to slow down and enjoy the sights around you.

Choosing the Wrong RV. There are various RVs to choose from, and you will absolutely find one that meets your needs. As we've discussed in detail, take the time to find the right fit. Don't rush into your RV purchase. Otherwise you might wind up with a model that is not fitted to your personal necessities and a whole lot of debt. Take your time to get everything right. After all, it is going to be your new home, and you'll be staying in it for quite a while, so you might as well make it a comfortable place to live in.

Forgetting to Retract the Awning. The awning is a versatile and useful part of the RV. However, it is also a fragile part that can be ruined by high winds and hard rains. If you suspect bad weather don't forget to bring in your awning.

Forgetting to Disconnect. This is something that happens more often than you may think. There is a lot you need to remember when packing up and leaving a campground. Find a way to remember to disconnect all utility lines before leaving. I personally recommend checklists or having your partner be someone with a great memory unless you already are that person and your partner gets to rest in that aspect.

Don't Be the Bad Neighbor. Always be conscious of those around you. Be quiet in the morning and evening hours. Pick up after yourself and your pets. RV parks and campgrounds are like small communities, and you want to make sure it is an enjoyable experience for everyone.

Forgetting to Level Your RV. Nothing is more uncomfortable than sleeping on an angle. Nothing is more difficult than constantly walking from one end of an RV to another at a slant. Both of these problems can be resolved easily by leveling. The process of leveling will depend on the type of RV you have. Never rely on the site to be level.

I lived in a slanted house for a time, and I can definitely ascertain it made my existence a bit more difficult and unstable in the process of adjusting between its crooked floors and the regular streets I walked on outside.

Overpacking. Even though you are living in your RV and are going to require a certain number of basic items, you should still avoid packing too much into your RV. From both space and weight standpoints, you have limits when it comes to what you get to keep.

Forgetting to Double Check. Before you leave to drive anywhere, you should always check and double check your RV. Check everything inside and out to save yourself a lot of problems down the road. Have a clear checklist, so you don't forget anything.

Forgetting to Defrost the Freezer. This may seem small, but it is easier to regularly defrost the refrigerator. If you allow ice to build up, it will cause the freezer to malfunction, and it will reduce precious storage space.

Not Taking the Time to Learn to Drive. As we talked about in the beginning, RVs are the same as cars only in the learning curve of driving them. You want to practice and take the time to get used to driving an RV before you head out on the road.

That is everything I've got. I've taught you all the insider points I know. Now you are truly ready to head out on the road and live the life you've always dreamed of. It may sound intimidating now that you know about the technical side of this plot twist in your existence. Like with many things you learn through a guide or book, practicing what you have gathered in the real world is both more complicated yet a lot simpler than you may have originally anticipated from only reading about it all.

This is why I greatly encourage you to try these tips and suggestions for yourself before reaching the conclusion of whether you want to live full-time in an RV or not, and who you would like to go on this adventure with. It is time you have your own adventure, whether it is traveling to Florence or visiting New Orleans in your trusty RV.

Regardless of where you go, you can count on enjoying yourself every step of the way if you choose to look at the positive outlook of any situation you are in. Happy trails.

LAST WORDS

I wanted to thank you for buying this book; we are neither a professional writer nor an author, but rather two people who always had the passion for travelling the country. In this book, I wanted to share our knowledge with you, as I know there are many people who share the same passion and drive as we do. So, this book is entirely dedicated to YOU my readers.

Despite our best effort to make this book error free, if you happen to find any errors, I want to ask for your forgiveness ahead of time.

Just remember, our writing skill may not be top notch, but the knowledge we share here is pure and honest.

If you thought we added some value and shared some valuable information that you can use, please take a minute and post a review on wherever you bought this book from. This will mean the world to us.

Thank you once again and be safe when travelling.

Made in the USA
Las Vegas, NV
02 February 2023

66717102R10188